# ALWAYS UPLIFTING

## A DAILY DEVOTIONAL TO LIGHTEN YOUR LOAD

## LISA WILT

~

*This book is dedicated to all YOU who share the light of Christ.*
*Together let's be "Always Uplifting."*

~

*Those who trust in the Lord will find new strength.*
*They will soar high on wings like eagles.*
*They will run and not grow weary.*
*They will walk and not faint.*
***Isaiah 40:31***

~

# INTRODUCTION

If you need a one-minute way to uplift your day, this devotional is for you. It can serve as caffeine for your soul every morning. Like a handful of Hershey's kisses, it can be a pick-me-up during your day when you're down. Or it can be used like a calming cup of chamomile tea at bedtime to help you relax and unwind focusing on God.

Each devotional is easy to read. Originally I wrote and recorded them for radio for listeners who are on the go and need to be uplifted to see Christ in the chaos not the devil in the details.

Life is busy so this book keeps it simple. With child-like faith together let's run to our Father to "find new strength and soar high on wings like eagles." So that we will "run and not grow weary" and "walk and not faint." That's my simple prayer. I promise this book will be "Always Uplifting!"

# MY FRIDGE AND MY LIFE

## MATTHEW 11:28-30

My fridge and my life have much in common. Both are filled yet I crave more. I crave meaning and purpose more than meat and potatoes. I long for more love and less leftovers. And sometimes I need help. Like the shelves of my fridge, my schedule becomes so crammed, I struggle to find what I need most. That's when I look to my Savior who says: "Come to me, all of you who are weary and carry heavy burdens and I will give you rest."

It's amazing what time spent resting in prayer with scripture can do for our sapped souls. That's why every page in this book has God's Word. His love can energize us more than chocolate or even caffeine. With His perspective we can relax, seeing our family's sticky fingerprints on the fridge as sweet blessings, rather than just something else that needs to be cleaned.

# PRAYER HOTLINE

## 1 THESSALONIANS 5:16-18

The Bible tells us to "pray without ceasing." That's three simple words that can simply change our lives. "Pray without ceasing." Prayer is a **hotline** that can become our **lifeline**. When we find ourselves waiting **in line**, we can pray. When we need **guidelines**, we can pray. When we are **declined** or **maligned**, we can pray.

When we need to be **streamlined** because we are up against a **timeline** and can't get **online**, we can pray. When we want to **recline** because we don't have enough energy to cross the **finish line**, we can pray.

When we're stuck on the **frontline** and we're inclined to give up, we can pray. Though our **hemlines, necklines** and **laugh lines** will certainly change, along with our home's **landlines**, we have a **prayer line** and a heavenly Father, who will always listen as we "pray without ceasing."

# MAKE A LIVING AND A LIFE

## COLOSSIANS 3:23-24

$\mathcal{W}$inston Churchill once said "We make a living by what we **get**, but we make a life by what we **give**."[1] For over thirty years I've made a living working as a pharmacist in the community and industry. In all honesty being a pharmacist was my dad's idea because it was a good job for a woman. It was not my first love. I loved to write. Yet God has taken what I like (science) and has allowed me to experience what I love (people).

And each year with the Holy Spirit's help my job becomes even better because it becomes more of a ministry serving others for His kingdom. I share this because I believe that no matter what work you do-whether you are a housekeeper or a popular speaker-when you ask God to work in and through you, your job becomes your gift to the world.

# WORCESTERSHIRE SAUCE

## PROVERBS 18:10

*I*t's been said that the three hardest things to say are "I was wrong." "I need help." And "Worcestershire Sauce." When we break words down, they're easier to pronounce. Worce-ster-shire. It's just three syllables, yet sometimes with me it comes out as five, "War-ces-ter-shy-er." As hard as it is to say, I find it's even harder to say that **I was wrong** and that **I need help**. When we're afraid and our world is crumbling, Proverbs 18:10 tells us: "The name of the Lord is a strong tower; the righteous run into it and are safe." So next time you need help, call out to Jesus. His name is easy to pronounce. Sometimes I pray it over and over, when no other words help.

Jesus.

Jesus.

Jesus.

There is power in His name!

# THE BIRTH OF A RAINBOW

PSALM 40:1-2

*T*he birth of a rainbow begins with trillions of tiny droplets. Colorless light enters each raindrop prism, then exits bent and broken into the seven splendid colors of the spectrum. Broken light becomes beautiful light.

The first rainbow was sent by God after The Flood to remind us of His promise to never again destroy the earth with water. God doesn't want us to fear each time raindrops fall into our lives. Likewise, God doesn't want us to fear when trials drop into our lives. **Rain can nourish life, just as trials can nourish faith.** Maybe you've been showered with trials, but always remember God pulls you and me from the "mud and the mire." He chooses us, wanting us to remember that He is trustworthy... even when spouses are not. He is faithful...even when friends are not. He is patient...even when we are not. And He loves us... even when we don't feel lovable.

# TIGHT PANTS

## PROVERBS 16:18

*S*tanding in front of the mirror in a pair of jeans that are too small doesn't make anyone feel happy about themselves. Today I realized that tight pants have a lot in common with pride. Neither make us look good.

While my old skinny jeans don't fit like they used to, they do make me think and ask myself a few uncomfortable questions like: "Has arrogance seeped into my thinking making me too big for my britches?" Do I respond in humility when I feel challenged or do I prayerfully consider another's opinion in relation to God's Word? When you look in the mirror next, consider a quote that I tried on for size from a man who had a BIG heart and a small ego. His mother called him William Franklyn, but we knew him as Billy Graham. He said: "We are the Bibles the world is reading; we are the creeds the world is needing; we are the sermons the world is heeding."

# ROMANCE AND DONUTS

## COLOSSIANS 3:12

*R*omance is like a donut. It tastes great, but without anything else, it doesn't satisfy. I hunger for something more filling than romance. I crave love and intimacy.

Intimacy is difficult to describe. Perhaps the purest definition is right before our eyes and can be found in the word itself. "In-to-me-see." Do you long to be truly seen with all your flaws and still loved unconditionally? I do.

Christ sees us and tells us in the Bible that nothing can separate us from His love. "Neither death nor life, neither angels nor demons, neither our fears for today nor our worries about tomorrow—not even the powers of hell can separate us from God's love." No other person sees us and understands us like Jesus does. Unlike a donut, His love can sustain and satisfy us forever.

# BALLOONS

## JAMES 2:14-24

They come in all colors, shapes and sizes. Some are as big as the Goodyear Blimp while others are as small as your fist. My preschooler still has her birthday balloon tied to the handlebars of her trike. It bobs back and forth, following her like a faithful friend. My son's gleaming eyes are glued.

As I watch them, I see that a balloon filled with air has a story to tell. Ordinarily air isn't something we see. But when it brings a balloon to life, we suddenly notice it. Air has much in common with faith. Faith is not something we ordinarily see. But when a person of faith shows extra-ordinary kindness, suddenly their faith becomes visible.

Balloons can bring others joy. I pray that my faith will bring others joy. Your faith can be made visible by your kind deeds. What might you do for someone today in Jesus's name?

## STUBBORN STAINS

1 JOHN 1:9

*S*tains are like bad memories. They're the blot left behind in my mind. While I do want to fully forgive, I find that the ugly memory is still hanging around–much like an ugly stain. And just like the stain, the memory often appears in the worst place at the worst time. Washing clothes once doesn't always completely remove the dirt and forgiving once doesn't always completely remove the hurt. Daily asking God to help me forgive is like pretreating a stain before it sets. God wants me to leave my disappointments and hurts with Him. He always listens and understands. He can shoulder the burden that I can't without becoming repressed, stressed and depressed. I have a long way to go in fully forgiving; but stains remind me that holding onto hurts and refusing to forgive leaves lingering, ugly memories. Fully forgiving others, as Christ forgives us, leaves us carefree, spotless and glimmering.

# A GOURMET JELLY BELLY®

## ROMANS 12:1-8

*U*nlike jelly beans that come in nine ordinary colors, Gourmet Jelly Belly® candies come in fifty extraordinary flavors like cotton candy and cappuccino. They can take up to fourteen days to make, which is why they're pricey.[1] Like the watermelon Jelly Belly® I just enjoyed, it looked like a little watermelon on the outside and tasted like a little watermelon on the inside. Unlike ordinary jelly beans that have the same sugary white interior, Jelly Bellies® are flavored through and through.

This reminds me that as Christians we are called to be like Jelly Bellies®. We are called to be flavored and transformed through and through so that others can see Christ in and through us. Like a buttered popcorn flavored Jelly Belly® I just popped in my mouth, how can you pop into someone's life today and uniquely flavor it with joy?

# LAWNS AND LIVES

## MATTHEW 6:30-34

*O*ur lawns have a lot in common with our lives! It's amazing how Spring rolls out the red carpet for the green grass. April has also ushered in some unwanted visitors. The dandelions were not invited. And the grass we hoped would R.S.V.P. to fill in the bare spots must have misplaced their invitations. Our perennials have a standing invitation, but several this year were no shows. Meanwhile, our shrubs are like old guests needing to be groomed.

Both my lawn and my life can become overgrown bushy with busyness! So how do we trim back weed-ridden schedules? Matthew 6:30-33 is like *Gardening 101:* "If God gives such attention to the appearance of wildflowers—most of which are never even seen—don't you think he'll attend to you?...What I'm trying to do here is to get you to relax, to not be so preoccupied with *getting*, so you can respond to God's *giving*."

# KINDERGARTEN & KINDNESS

ACTS 9:36-41

On Fridays my mom would pick me up from kindergarten on her bicycle. Dad had welded a tractor seat on the back. The breeze would blow my hair as we rode without helmets to the donut shop one block away.

There I would climb onto a swirly bar stool and spin as I breathed in the sweet air. With school behind me and donuts before me, my soul dripped with happiness like Long Johns dripped with warm icing. I was allowed to order three donut holes and chocolate milk with an accordion straw. To this day I still smile fondly whenever I see donut holes, little cartons of milk or bendable straws. And when given an option, I always chosse a swiveling stool over a more conventional chair.

Donut holes and a miniature carton of chocolate milk are small things. When we were in **kind**ergarten we learned to be **kind**. What small kindness can you share today?

# OVER TWO TRILLION STEPS

## JOSHUA 6:1-17

*J*oshua fought the battle of _____ and the walls came tumbling down. We know the story well and can fill in the blank. We remember the victory but we often forget that this win came after a forty-year journey that should've only taken forty days.

When I feel uncertain and stuck, I've been known to pray that God would miraculously bring barriers tumbling down. What I forget is that Joshua and his 40,000 soldiers circled Jericho every day for six days and on the seventh day, they circled it seven times. (That's thirteen times.) Each time they circled, each soldier took roughly 6,000 steps. So the victory was won with over two trillion steps of obedience! For me the biggest lesson buried in the tumbled walls is to take the first God-directed step of faith...then the next...and the next. What step of faith is God inviting you to take today?

# TOMATOES

JOHN 17:21-23

ou say to-maw-toe. I say to-may-toe. You say catsup. I say ketchup. We can focus on our differences and build fences or we can focus on our likenesses and discover gates. Liking others makes them easier to love and we each are called to love our neighbor.

Surely we could find more likenesses if we looked. We are each children of God and are sinners saved by grace. We each need love. And we need hope to survive every bit as much as we need oxygen to breath. We each crave meaning and purpose even more than meat and potatoes.

We are sons and daughters, moms and dads, spouses and siblings, coworkers and countrymen. So let's look for likenesses as we all agree that to-may-toes and to-maw-toes are the main ingredient in catsup and ketchup.

## MOTHER-IN-LAWS AND FEAR

### JOHN 14:27-31

"*F*ear not." It's the most repeated command from the lips of Jesus and is found in every book in the Bible. It appears 365 times-one for every day of the year-because fear visits everyone.

Yet the presence of fear does not mean you have no faith. Even Jesus had moments when He was afraid. I believe that's why Jesus's parting words were: "Peace is what I leave with you; it is my own peace that I give you. I do not give it as the world does. Do not be worried and upset: do not be afraid!"

Like a mother-in-law, fear may visit your home but fear does NOT have a permanent invitation to stay. As Corrie Ten Boom, who survived the Nazi concentration camp, reminds us: "Never be afraid to trust an **unknown** future to a **known** God."[1] God does not want us to live with fear. Fears, tears and mother-in-laws need healthy boundaries.

# P.B.J.'S

## MATTHEW 22:36-40

*P*eanut butter was once considered a delicacy as it takes nearly 550 peanuts to make one jar. Way back in 1901 the first peanut butter and jelly sandwich recipe appeared in the *Boston Cooking School Magazine of Culinary Science.*[1]

Now everyone knows how to make a PBJ. Anyone of any age on any budget can take it anywhere and eat it any time. No recipe or refrigeration required. A PBJ is oh so good yet oh so simple.

Sometimes when it comes to our faith, we need to get back to the basics. Like a PBJ, Jesus keeps it simple. He summarizes all 613 commands telling us to simply love God and love others. Love never ends and love always wins! Like a PBJ, that's a great recipe for living.

# POOL TABLE OR PARKING LOT?

## HEBREWS 4:16

*I*t's every parent's nightmare. The phone call that your teen has been in a high speed crash. My folks got that call the day I lost control of the family sedan and nearly lost my life in a head-on collision. At 65 MPH I swerved off the highway and into a new car lot. Like a billiard ball on a pool table, I crashed into five colorful new trucks lined up on the front row before my little Maverick stalled out between two crumpled sedans. I demolished seven vehicles in seven seconds. While I may have deserved a ticket, my dad saw things differently through eyes of grace. I was a puddle of tears. He was a pillar of strength. Might you remember a time when someone saved you from a mess you had made, extending love instead of judgement? If so, grace has colored your life. Which brings me back to the colorful cars I crunched. Have you ever told the person who rescued you how much you appreciate them?

# CHANGING THE WORLD

## JAMES 2:14-20

he world is changed by our example not by our opinion.[1] Helping one person might not change the whole world, but it could change the world for that one person. The Bible tells us whatever we do for the least of our brothers, it is as if we have done that for Jesus.

Sometimes the least of our brothers cut us off on the highway. Sometimes they cut us off mid-sentence in a conversation. Sometimes they work for the help desk and cut us off placing us back on hold before we can explain our computer glitch.

Lots of times they have different skin colors, cultural biases and political views. They may worship God differently and have different religious experiences. While we will never change the world by *going to church*, we can change the world by *being the church*. After all, the world is not changed by our opinion. The world is changed by our example.

# SAVORY AND SWEET

## EPHESIANS 4:26-27

*H*ickory peach ice cream with candied bacon topping. Never tried it, but the picture of it sure looks yummy! Savory and sweet go well together just like "I love you" and "I am sorry."

My husband and I have different personalities. He's more savory and I'm more sweet so we have our disagreements. But the Bible tells us, "don't sin by letting anger control you. And don't let the sun go down while you are still angry." This is my favorite verse to write inside wedding cards because it's wisdom that has helped me through the ups and downs of marriage.

Holding grudges while withholding apologies make sleeping hard. I know because I have earned my masters from U.T.T. (the University of Toss and Turn). So like ice cream before bedtime, why not try "I love you and I am sorry." They make a perfect pair to get past your past.

# BATTLES TO BLESSINGS

## GENESIS 22:1-18

*A*sk God to turn your worries to worship so that your battles can become blessings. When you and I worry, we focus on **the problem**. When we pray, we focus on **the Provider**. One of God's many names is Jehovah-Jireh or "the Lord will provide." In Hebrew the word "provide" also means "to see to it."[1]

When Abraham calls God Jehovah-Jireh, he is saying, you see and experience all this need of mine and make provision for it. Like a father caring for his only son, it is deeply personal.

God provided a lamb as a substitute sacrifice for Abraham's son Issac. This foreshadowed the perfect Lamb of God who sacrificed His life for the forgiveness of our sins. We can trust God to provide. When we give God our worries and worship Him, He can turn our faith battles into faith blessings!

# VITAMINS, JEWELRY AND JESUS

JOHN 6:35-40

My daughter insists "Vitamins are good for my tummy!" Alyssa prefers vitamins over vegetables any day. But are vitamins a substitute or a supplement–an accessory or an essential? Like jewelry is an accessory to our outfits, vitamins are an accessory to our diets. Carbs, proteins and fats are dietary essentials like shirts, pants and shoes are clothing essentials. I've forgotten to wear my ring, but I've never forgotten to wear my pants! When you're hungry you don't go to the medicine cabinet for a plate of vitamins, you go to the kitchen cabinet for a plate of food. Just as we have basic nutritional needs, we have basic spiritual needs. The Father, Son and Holy Spirit are essential like proteins, carbs and fats.

When your spirit is starved and you have an emptiness that food can't fill, Jesus promises: "I am the bread of life. Whoever comes to me will never be hungry again!" Come to Jesus today.

# LUKEWARM LOPSIDED LOVE

## REVELATION 3:15-16

*S*tarbucks has 87,000 coffee combinations.[1] They've taken coffee choices to new levels of complexity. But even with 87,000 options, Starbucks serves coffee either steaming hot or ice cold. Even worse than lukewarm coffee is lukewarm love. When someone we love acts lukewarm or indifferent, it hurts us. Likewise, when we act lukewarm or indifferent to God, it hurts Him. God tells us that nothing will ever separate us from His love. Yet sometimes we move away from Him. That's when these questions may be helpful.

Do I delight in my quiet time with God or am I more excited to talk to a friend at Starbucks?

Do I have consistent time in His Word or am I more consistent in my coffee habit?

Do I rely on His Spirit to pick me up as much as I rely on caffeine to pick me up?

# MY CRISPER DRAWER

## GALATIANS 5:16-26

*I* never realized until today that refrigerator crisper drawers have humidity settings. Since we moved into our home adopting the old left-behind fridge, our setting has been parked indecisively in the middle. I don't know about your crisper drawer, but mine should be called a "rotter drawer." The problem is that you can just shut the drawer so you don't have to feel guilty when you grab for the jar of ice cream topping. Sometimes I have the spiritual equivalent of a rotter drawer in my life. I have apples of anger, grapes of gossip, pears of pride, grapefruits of greed, radishes of resentment, celery of selfishness, lemons of lust, and putrefied potatoes of pessimism. Perhaps you and I need to ask the Holy Spirit to replace our rotten, forgotten, fleshy fruit with fresh, spiritual fruit. "The Holy Spirit produces this kind of fruit in our lives: love, joy, peace, patience, kindness, goodness, faithfulness, gentleness, and self-control."

# WHAT COLOR IS GRACE?

JOHN 8:12

*I*f you had to describe grace with a color using only your eyes, what color would you choose? When I close my eyes and picture grace, I think of God and bright, white light. Did you know that white light has every color of the spectrum in it? It's true. All the different wavelengths of color cancel each other so light becomes radiant white.

This reminds me of God's grace. It cancels all our sins just as all the other wavelengths cancel color making white light brightest. Through Christ we are as bright as pure light.

Bright light warms us like sunshine, just as God's love warms our spirits. Jesus said: "I am the light of the world. Whoever follows me will never walk in darkness but will have the light of life." How can you brighten someone's day in your own way today?

# TEETER-TOTTERS

## ROMANS 12:1-8

*W*e each remember the backyard we had while growing up. When I was a kid, I thought we had the best yard on the block. The feature attraction was the teeter-totter that went up and down and even twirled around. Like everything else, my Dad made it out of old parts.

I take after my dad. One of my greatest pleasures is to make something new out of something old. I've also learned that my Heavenly Father is the Master at restoring. He created us, so He knows our talents. He multiplies our gifts so that we have an abundance to share.

What you may think is an ordinary skill can become extra-ordinary and multiplied in His hands. Whatever we have, we can use for His glory. Like my dad did when he made our cool teeter-totter, can you vow to bless those "up and down and around" you?

# A WEE LITTLE MAN

## LUKE 19:1-10

We all know that "Zacchaeus was a wee little man and a wee little man was he. He climbed up in a sycamore tree for the Lord he wanted to see." I love this story because it gives us a peek inside the heart of Jesus. Zacchaeus fell short. He was a short man, who was short-sighted, and would short other when collecting trumped-up taxes.

But Jesus looked at what Zacchaeus could become not what he had been. Just as Jesus saw Zacchaeus, He sees you. And just as He called Zacchaeus by name, Jesus is calling you by name.

You may feel short on time. And there may be times you fall short, have a short fuse and short circuit. Fearful times when you kept others on a short leash and were short-sighted.

You may feel like you're one sandwich short of a picnic, but you're not. Jesus wants to be invited into your house and heart today!

# DON'T ICE BURNT CAKE

## PROVERBS 12:22

"If the cake is burnt, don't ice it and please don't ask me to eat it." This is my way of saying, I don't want the sugar-coated truth that may sound better but taste bitter. Taking a note from Jesus who told great stories, I once burnt a cupcake and iced it. Placing it on a pretty plate, I asked for a meeting with my boss. He had just rolled out a plan that was advantageous for the company but NOT for employees.

I used the cupcake, which he assumed was a treat for him, to speak for me by simply stating: "If something is burnt, please don't ice it and ask others to eat it." This set the tone for an honest discussion to follow.

God values honesty too. His Word tells us: "The Lord delights in those who tell the truth." So today, and every day, let's speak the truth in love and in a way that others can digest.

# MORE THAN MERCY

LUKE 15:11-32

God grants us grace and mercy. Both are good but is one better? If given the choice, I would always choose grace over mercy. Grace is God's idea and it's more than mercy. Mercy gives a granola bar and a few bucks to someone who is homeless and hungry. Grace invites them home for dinner and gives them the guest bedroom. Mercy accepts the apology of the prodigal child. Grace gives them a royal robe, a ring for their finger and throws a party with the fatted calf.

We each need mercy but God gives us more. He gives us grace "new every morning." He throws us a party and welcomes us home no matter how long we've been gone or how far we have wandered. Whether you're a prodigy (wonderfully extraordinary) or a prodigal (wastefully extravagant) or someone in between (like me), you are your Father's child. God is waiting, watching the horizon, longing to welcome you home.

# BILLIARD BALLS AND EASTER EGGS

LUKE 15:8-10

My toddler loves Easter egg hunts. And since Daddy's billiard balls looked like her Easter eggs, she hid them. That was weeks ago. The eight ball is still missing.

This leads me to ask: Have you ever lost something that's important to you? In the Bible we can read the story of a woman who had ten coins until one turned up missing. She looked everywhere and when she found it, she celebrated. Jesus tells us that God's angels throw a party every time one lost soul finds Him.

So the next time you're frustrated searching for **something** that is lost, can you pray for **someone** who is lost? Your time will be well spent because people are infinitely more important than things.

# A GOWN BUT NO GROOM

JOHN 14:28-31

*H*e proposed! She accepted! Joyful engagement photos were taken. Save-the-date cards were sent. With her mom by her side, Sofia said yes to the dress.

Then this bride-to-be was diagnosed with lupus and found herself with a gown but no groom.

Maybe you've never experienced a broken engagement, but have you ever experienced a broken heart? Sometimes life is lonely and hurts. Jesus knew this. So before He left this Earth, He sent us His Spirit to be our Friend and Comforter.

In John 14 He promises, "I'm leaving you well and whole. My parting gift to you is peace. I don't leave you the way you're used to being left—feeling abandoned." So while fiancés may flee from fear, know that the Holy Spirit is always with you. Never will He leave or forsake you for someone who is healthier, prettier, smarter or richer! He loves you with all your imperfections.

# TWO GOLDFISH CRACKERS & FIVE CROUTONS

## MATTHEW 14:13-21

*H*ave you ever had less than you needed and you needed God to show up? I sure have. Today I was reading the miracle of Jesus feeding 5,000 men with two fish and five loaves. And what struck me is that He feeds us and others by asking us to give Him what we have. He wants our *ordinary* five-loaves-and-two-fish abilities and moments.

Sometimes it feels like we have only two goldfish crackers and five croutons and everyone around us wants a big bite. But our talents and time in God's hands is enough and can make a difference. It may not seem like much compared to the need, but He starts with the *ordinary*. He never asks for more than you and I have, but He wants us to trust Him to multiply **what we have** to meet **what others need**. Just as He did when He fed 5,000, He made the *ordinary* **extra-ordinary**. What do you need most today and what do you have that you can share?

# MIRAGES AND JOY

JAMES 1:1-12

*A*s you're driving on a scorching day, have you ever seen what appears to be water on the highway's horizon and wondered why? What we see are heat waves rising up from the road. And as we move closer, the water seemingly moves farther away.

Just as we never experience driving through the puddle, some never experience lasting joy. Joy is distant and elusive like a mirage.

Jesus understands that work can be scorching, kids can be draining, and relationships can have dry spells. And that's exactly when you and I need to turn to Him and His Word most. When it is sweltering, heat waves appear to remind us that—unlike mirages—His joy lies just ahead and is just as real as what lies beyond the horizon.

# TWO-OUNCE TONGUES

## PSALM 19:14

*I*t seems everyone wants to lose a few pounds so let's talk about tongues. When our tongue's taste buds scream for more, we indulge. Our tongues weigh about two ounces but they can sure weigh us down. It's hard to control our weight and even harder to control our words. I need God's help with both. While my tongue is light, it can lead to heavy hurts. So rather than let words fly when tempers flare, I've been using my tongue to pray Psalm 19 that ends like this, "May the words of my mouth and the meditations of my heart be pleasing in your sight, O Lord, my Rock and my Redeemer."

While our tongue is a small muscle, it's strong and can speak in faith to move mountains. Heavy words weigh us down but uplifting words lift us up. What words of encouragement can you speak into someone's life today that will move mountains of fear for them?

# YOUR WORST SCHOOL PICTURE

## 2 CORINTHIANS 12:8-10

*G*rowing up we all had a least one horrible school picture. What did yours look like and what made it so bad? When I was eleven, I chipped my front tooth as I was sprinting inside to grab a call from my cousin Kimmy. I remember pushing myself up on my bloodied elbows and being horrified to see half of my front tooth lying on the brick.

Now years later people compliment me on my smile saying it's one of my best features. Funny how God can take what we think is marred and make it beautiful. If you have experienced this personally, this is your testimony.

God can take our upside-down moments (when we quite literally fall landing face down on a brick) and turn them right side up. He can take the bad and make it better. God can embrace what we think is a weakness and transform it into a strength.

# DONUTS WITH SPRINKLES

## PHILIPPIANS 4:4-9

*L*ike children, donuts bring delight. At three my daughter loves any "doughny" with sprinkles. She is convinced the pink sprinkles taste the sweetest. She bounces and announces, "the more sprinkles, the more yummier!"

As adults sometimes our responsibilities are so heavy that it's hard to be lighthearted about small blessings like sprinkles on donuts. I could learn a lot from my kiddos about delight.

And I can learn a lot from God's Word that tells us: "Fix your thoughts on what is true, honorable, right, pure, lovely, admirable, excellent and worthy of praise." These are the sprinkles that make life "more yummier." So if you have a container of sprinkles, set it out in your kitchen as a reminder to see the colorful blessings that God sprinkles throughout your day.

# INVISIBLE OR INDIVISIBLE?

## JOHN 17:21-24

Over dinner tonight my daughter shared exciting news from preschool. "I got to hold the 'frag' today!" This is an honor as only one student is chosen each day. Alyssa is proud to share her accomplishment as she holds up her fork as if it were the flag. She respectfully clutches her throat rather than covering her heart and begins: "I pledge allegiance to the 'frag'..."

She's on a roll until she hits, "One nation, under God, invisible..." We share that the word is "in**di**visible," but she insists with the confidence of Moses: "God is invisible!" Then as if to calm our fears she adds, "but He's not 'ascary.'"

Though she doesn't have the perfect vocabulary, she does know God isn't frightening. He's a loving Father. And though she doesn't know the word "indivisible," we can teach our children by example to be indivisible and united in Christ!

# BROWNIES, REVENGE AND REFUGE

## 1 PETER 3:9-12

*E*ating a pan of brownies feels good while we're doing it, but afterward...not so much. I've heard it said, "revenge is sweet." Like a batch of brownies, revenge may taste sweet at first but God offers a healthier alternative.

The Bible tells us "do not repay evil for evil. Don't retaliate with insults when people insult you. Instead, pay them back with a blessing. That is what God has called you to do, and he will grant you his blessing."

This verse tells me that instead of seeking **revenge**, I should seek **re**fuge in God. Psalm 91 promises that God will be our refuge and our fortress. Together we can trust Him to defend us and to bring perfect justice. Regret feels horrible like a tight pair of jeans after we've eaten an entire batch of brownies.

# THE TENDERIZER

## EPHESIANS 4:31-32

*B*edtime traditions from childhood are some of the sweetest memories. My Dad would tuck my siblings and me in bed by "tenderizing" us. He used the sides of his hands to "karate chop" us faster than a drum roll from head to toe and back again. It vibrated every last giggle from our tired little bodies.

Back then I thought that no one could top my Dad at "tenderizing." Now I understand that my heavenly Father is the best "Tenderizer" because He can soften hardened hearts.

If you know someone that seems cynical, unapproachable and determined to avoid God, Christ can work miracles in quiet corners of their heart. I've seen it happen in my own family. So keep praying. God will never give up on them because He loves them dearly!

# GUINNESS BOOK OF WORLD RECORDS AND HOPE

## 2 CORINTHIANS 4:16-18

*B*elieve it or not a person can hold their breath twice as long if they inhale pure oxygen first. The Guinness Book of World Records for breath holding underwater is about eleven minutes. When given pure oxygen first, the world record is doubled to over twenty-two minutes underwater.[1]

Just as our brain needs oxygen, our soul needs hope. Like oxygen, hope helps us not only survive but to thrive. But how and where do we find hope in a fallen world? Here's a few paths I've walked that can lead you home to HOPE.

- **H-H**is Word: **Hymns. Godly books. Sermons.**
- **O-O**thers: Pastors. Godly friends. Mentors.
- **P-**Putting others first: Serving with your gifts.
- **E-**Earth: Pets and sunsets. Seeing our Creator in Creation.

# CRAYONS AND HEAVEN

## REVELATION 21:1-7

Picking out school supplies can be so much fun! Growing up my favorite purchase was the BIG box of sixty-four Crayolas® with the sharpener built in. To have new crayons seemed like a sliver of heaven. But after the first week, only colors like Bittersweet and Raw Sienna still had perfect points. Even at five I didn't want my family of five stick people to live in the bittersweet world of raw sienna.

While every day on this earth is smudged with some imperfection, every tear cried today can serve as a rainbow promise of sorts. Tears can remind us of the day in heaven when there will be no more tears, when nothing will taste bittersweet and when no hurts will be raw.

My prayer is that knowing this can help us journey through the less than perfect days, finding joy in the fact that through Jesus, you and I are destined for a heavenly, happily ever after!

# A GOAT NAMED KUBOTA

## GALATIANS 6:9

*B*razen. Belligerent. Bold. Thieves broke into our barn and went on a shopping spree. They filled up the bed of our little truck with tools like it was Santa's sleigh. I wondered if they might come back to rob our home next.

Rather than be a **fearful worrier**, I asked God to help me be a **faithful warrior**. While my husband installed a security camera, I wrote the date in my Bible with a fine Sharpie® and simple prayer: "Father, please take my fear, build Dave's faith and, if You see fit, return our Kubota."

Five days later our little truck was found. In gratitude I bought a goat through World Vision for a third-world family. So the next time you are harmed or wronged, ask God to exchange your fear for faith. God can use what hurt you to help others. Your story of restoration may not result in a goat, but it's sure to be great!

# PAIN AND THE PIANO

ROMANS 8:28-29

*I*f you chop off the "o" and shuffle the vowels, "piano" spells "pain." Growing up, piano lessons brought me pain. Dad and Mom wanted music to color my life. Instead I dreaded lessons because my teacher was gritty. The thought of her glaring disappointment struck fear in my heart. My hands obeyed but my soul never sang.

When my sister accidentally rode her bike over my head leaving a tire imprint, I got out of lessons. This nasty accident on the side of the highway with our new bicycles was less painful than a half hour lesson with Mrs. Moberly.

While piano spelled pain for me, maybe something else spelled pain for you growing up. Whatever it may be, together we can pray the promise that, "God, who makes everything work together, will work all things into his most excellent harmonies." God can heal our painful memories.

# BOOMERANGS

## GALATIANS 5:22-25

*B*eing in control feels great. While we all would like to control our circumstances, most of us are still trying to master "self-control" especially when we are emotionally hot and angry. Self-control or "temperance" is a fruit of the Holy Spirit living in us.

I like the word "temperance" because it takes "self" out of the equation. "Self" or my mouth usually gets me in trouble. There are thousands of self-help books on self-control in the self-improvement section of book stores for self study. When I am emotionally hot, I need less of myself and more of His Spirit.

We are told in *Ecclesiastes 7:9: "Don't be quick to fly off the handle. Anger boomerangs. You can spot a fool by the lumps on his head." With the help of God's Spirit, my heart needs to soften and my spiritual fruit ripen so that my hard head is less lumpy.

# AN ARM AND A LEG

PSALM 139:13-18

*I* would give an arm and a leg to be _____. We each would fill in the blank differently. When I was in grade school, I came home complaining that my legs were fat compared to slender Susie Stuckey's legs.

My mom told me I had beautiful legs and reminded me to be grateful that my legs worked. Then she added with unwavering conviction, "Lisa, you're fearfully and wonderfully made. Do not criticize God's creation."

While I didn't thank God for my curves back then, I have never forgotten my mom's wisdom. Who are we to criticize God for making us each different? Next time you look in the mirror, might you remind yourself that you're wonderfully made and thank your Creator who loves you dearly?

# BELLY BUTTONS

## JOHN 15:4-17

*W*hen my daughter was playing in the bathtub she wondered out loud: "Mommy, what are belly buttons for?" I answered: "When you were in my tummy, that's where your umbilical cord was connected. Before you were born, Mommy fed you through that cord like you drink milk through a straw. That's how you grew to be so beautiful."

This got me thinking. What are belly buttons good for once we're born? Well, maybe they can remind us that just as we were once connected to our earthly mother for nourishment, we now need to stay connected to our heavenly Father for nourishment.

I've found that staying connected to God sometimes requires disconnecting from things like the internet and our cell phones. Like a vine stays connected to a branch, Jesus tells us that those who stay connected to Him will bear much fruit. So no matter what is on your schedule today, take and make time to abide.

# TO INFINITY AND BEYOND

## EPHESIANS 3:18-21

"To infinity and beyond!" That's how much God loves you. This phrase was spoken by Buzz Lightyear from *Toy Story*. But it reminds me of more important words spoken by Paul to describe God's love for us.

Paul prays that we will have, "the power to understand how wide, how long, how high, and how deep God's love is though it is too great to fully understand. Through his mighty power at work within us, we can accomplish **infinitely** more than we might ask or think." So these verses remind us that with His love we can go "to infinity and beyond."

No matter what age or stage in life, just like the theme song from Toy Story, Jesus promises, "You've Got a Friend in Me." So when life knocks you down, kneel down then look up knowing your are infinitely important to your Father and you are infinitely loved.

# ETCH A SKETCH®

## 1 CORINTHIANS 15:54-58

*Y*ou never forget how to use an Etch A Sketch®. The simplicity of just two dials is refreshing. An Etch A Sketch is fueled by metal shavings and a modest magnet. No batteries needed. Stop counting the required bytes.

The simplicity of the magnetic Etch A Sketch® reminds me of the simplicity of the magnetic message of salvation. Not only does Jesus save us from spiritual death, but He also saves us from the fear of death. We learn in 1 Corinthians 15 that: "Death is swallowed by triumphant life. Who got the last word, oh, Death? Who's afraid of you now?"

When I was younger, the thought of death was scary. Know that you're not alone if you are fearful. But also know you can give those anxieties to Jesus. He can erase fear like you can erase an Etch a Sketch®.

# BARBEQUE POTATO CHIPS

## ROMANS 7:14-25

*I*t's tough to resist the urge to splurge! I vividly remember the day I ate my first barbecue potato chip. I was sitting on the front step of my best friend's house next door. Honestly, I didn't eat just one chip but rather I ate Laura's whole bag. Now I understand why my mom never bought chips. Appetites for food, romance, excitement, beauty and money can hurl perpetual, fleshy temptations. I picture this spiritual struggle as a teeter-totter, like the one my dad built when I was a kid. If my big sister was down, I was up.

The same is true in the struggle with the flesh. When one is in control, the other is out of control. That's why we struggle with ups and downs. So while I still occasionally slip up and chow down on chips, I now buy a small bag of chips and a large bag of baby carrots. With the Holy Spirit's help is there a solution that could help you in a specific battle of the flesh?

# TIMING AND ORDER

## JOHN 11:1-44

Matthew, Mark, Luke and John. We expect the four gospels to be in that order. It just sounds backward to say John, Luke, Mark and Matthew even though that puts them in alphabetical order. This makes me think.

So often God's order or timing in our lives is not what we expect and seems backward. That's certainly how Mary and Martha felt when Jesus arrived after their brother Lazarus had been dead for three days. They had sent word and prayed that He would come sooner so He could heal Lazarus.

Like Mary and Martha, I can feel disappointed and become angry with Jesus. I can be impatient when I pray, favoring fast results. But God reassures me that He is in control and His timing is perfect. Even though His order and timing may be difficult for us to understand and accept, He sees the big picture and wants us to trust Him!

# DIAMONDS

## ISAIAH 43:1-4

*A* diamond is brilliant and beautiful but it certainly doesn't start that way. Like a lump of coal, a diamond is made of carbon. Yet after thousands of years with millions of pounds of pressure, carbon emerges transformed. It's a dull diamond in the rough. But the diamond cutter sees how the gem could sparkle.

Likewise, God is our Master Artisan. Every life experience imparts dimension. We may question why God allows health crises, hardships and heartaches. If given the choice, we might choose an easy, comfortable life over a hard one. But diamonds aren't formed under comfortable conditions.

We are multifaceted, beloved, brilliant and beautiful in God's eyes. There are millions of diamonds but only one you. So shine on dear friend, shine on!

# ARE YOU SALTY?

## MATTHEW 5:13-16

It's the night before Thanksgiving and there's a hush before the flurry of family arrives. Today I spent the day slicing, dicing, salting and tasting in preparation for the dozens of dishes that make the day so delectably yummy.

Now it's nearly midnight. As I sit in silence sipping on sleepy-time tea, I stare at my long list of recipes and notice that they all have one ingredient in common. Each contains salt; it's the most common seasoning used all over the world since the beginning of time.

Salt brings out flavor, making sweets sweeter and sauces more savory. Perhaps that's why Jesus tells us to be the salt of the Earth. We are here to love others…to enhance and preserve and to bring out the good. So together let's be "salt of the earth" friends who make every season sweeter.

# HOSPITALS AND HOSPITALITY

LUKE 14:12-14

The Louvre. The Eiffel Tower. The Taj Mahal. And The Great Wall. These are the destinations that fill bucket lists. Yet none are as expensive to stay per day as the last place we will likely visit. Hospitals.

While hospitals scare us, hospitality comforts us. Hospitality helps us feel safe and secure. It's something that everyone wants in all the places they go and from all the people they see. Having worked in hospitals for nearly thirty-five years, I can tell you that in the hospital along with medicine, hospitality helps heal.

The Statue of Liberty. The Sydney Opera House. And The Grand Canyon. They are all great, but none are as grand as a heart that offers hospitality. So no matter where your bucket list takes you, God is already there. And while hospitals may be one of the last places you visit, you can leave a legacy of hospitality by loving others today.

# SILK, STEEL & TRAILS

## JAMES 1:2-4

*S*ilk and steel have a lot in common. Both are strong, yet pound for pound, silk is actually stronger than steel. I love the feel of sheer silk. And I have to smile knowing it's stronger than its weight in steel. Since silk is lightweight, it's perfect for body armor for officers and soldiers.[1]

Go figure. Silk from a silkworm that starts its life trapped inside a hard coccoon can help protect police officers with body armor made from their silk strands. That's such a God thing… silky soft yet strong as steel.

Today I was reading in the Bible that we are to consider hard trials a "sheer" gift because trials make us stronger and more resilient. So while I effortlessly appreciate soft silk, I am learning to appreciate hard trials that strengthen me and build endurance. Together with God, our lives can be a beautiful gift like silk…strong yet soft!

# GOOGLE AND GOD

## ROMANS 12:1-8

*8*,400,000 Google searches will be performed just while you read this page. The average American turns to Google nearly four times a day with questions.[1] This makes me wonder, how many times each day do we turn to God and His Word? Surely Google **informs** us but God's Word **transforms** us.

The Bible tells us that we are not to be conformed to the world, rather we are to be transformed to think and look like Christ. Then we will know what is good and pleasing to God, better understanding what to do in difficult struggles. We will fulfill God's plan for our lives and understand why we were created. Our lives will have meaning and purpose leaving a legacy of love. We become new creations with a twinkle in our eye and excitement in our voice. So while Google can **inform** us and the world can **conform** us, God's Word can **transform** us into stars that shine bright.

# DELIGHT, DESIRES & DECEPTION

## PSALM 37:1-8

*J*f Bible verses were in a popularity contest, this one might win: "Take delight in the Lord, and he will give you the desires of your heart." In fact, it inspired me to write an entire book about delight.

So often our focus is on the last half of this verse, but our desires can deceive us. Perhaps that's why we are told to delight in God so He can give us the right desires rather than just palpable things…like spouses and houses. While neither of these are bad, a desire is a craving not a thing.

When the psalmist tells us to "delight in the Lord" we know where to go because we are told to seek God first and all other things will be given to us. We will never exhaust the delight God has planned for us…not in a lifetime. We have all eternity to live in pure delight and enjoy our heavenly happily ever after.

# THE P.U.S. MAN

MATTHEW 19:26

*B*etween meals to be made and bills to be paid, sometimes I lose my temper and my perspective. Today I asked for my daughter's forgiveness and explained that Momma needed a time-out...alone. Wanting to be helpful, Alyssa offered, "I go see Nana. The P.U.S. man can take me." She insists the nice U.P.S. man who rings the doorbell and delivers our packages is the P.U.S. man.

Like Alyssa, sometimes I get things more important than letters out of order. Instead of praying first, so that God can break the problem down like a cardboard box, I pray after I've tried to package problems up and ship them off. I try to accomplish everything by myself. Often I'm overwhelmed with tasks that are big and heavy, like the boxes the U.P.S. man delivers. At those times I am encouraged by the promise that "those things that are impossible for us are possible with God."

# A DUMBFOUNDING PAIR

## ECCLESIASTES 3:1-8

*W*ho doesn't love deals that are steals? One evening as we were finishing dinner, I gave my son shoes that I had bought at a **Buy-One-Get-One** sale. He took one look and declared, "those look like tug boats!" Over the years I have hit many shoe sales, but I've never bought just one shoe. Just as shoes come in pairs, I have found that often a **joy** is paired with a **sorrow**, a **success** is paired with a **setback** or a **delight** is paired with a **disappointment**. **Good** and **bad**. They are a dumbfounding pair. Slowly I am learning to see struggles as I see **Buy One Get One** sales. Sometimes when I shop for joy, I receive sorrow paired with it. As I walk in faith, God is teaching me to savor the sweet. And the sour? He's teaching me to see those things from His perspective...to trust that He is trustworthy when He promises me that He will bring good even out of those things that are bad.

# LET'S GET F.A.T. TOGETHER

## LUKE 16:10-12

*L*et's get fat together. F.A.T. is an acronym. It was used to describe Billy Graham at his funeral by his youngest son Ned Graham.

- The **F** reminds us to be FAITHFUL.
- The **A** reminds us to be AVAILABLE.
- The **T** reminds us to be TEACHABLE.

In 1 Timothy 4:8 we learn that, "Physical training is good, but training for godliness is much better, promising benefits in this life and in the life to come."

Surely we can be spiritually F.A.T. while being physically fit. So here's to being FAITHFUL, AVAILABLE and TEACHABLE together as we share the uplifting love of Jesus every day!

# THE MOMENT

## JOHN 10:10

*L*ive **in** the moment not **for** the moment. We don't live for the moment because living for the moment can lead to choices we regret. But we can live in the moment. Fully alive and fully present. How do we do that? We follow Jesus.

He's our Good Shepherd who watches over us. He leads us beside still waters to drink. This image is important because when sheep drink from rushing waters, their wool coats get wet weighing them down and pulling them under. Like sheep, our Good Shepherd knows the same can happen to us.

Currents of worry can pull us in and heavy temptations can weigh us down. We can drown in regret. But Jesus came to save us so that we might have "life and life to the fullest." With our Good Shepherd we can live **in** the moment, not **for** the moment.

# BEDOUINS AND A HALF-FULL GLASS

PSALM 62:5-8

*H*aving a glassful rather than a glass half full sure sounds better! Recently on my trip to the Holy Land, I met Bedouin nomadic shepherds. Despite being dirt poor living in tin shanties in the desert, they're known for their extravagant hospitality. While they'd never ask a stranger to leave, they have an interesting custom. It's said that if a Bedouin gives you a full cup of water, it's their way to communicate that their home is full with no room for you. If they give you a half cup of water, it's communicates they have plenty of room for you and it's your invitation to stay. Here in America, we think that full is better than half full. Like our glasses, we tend to fill our schedules full as well. Now might you think differently about the glass which represents your day, knowing that free space may allow you to have more time for those you love? Perhaps having a glass half full is better!

# I AM WHO I AM

## EXODUS 3:14-15

When asked His name God said, "**I am** who **I am**." It's hard for me to get my arms around such an epic answer and fully understand it. So God sent down-to-earth Jesus who spoke our language saying: "**I am** the bread of life...**I am** the Light of the world...**I am** the gate...I am the good shepherd...**I am** the way, the truth and the life...**I am** the resurrection and the life."

Then Jesus tells us in the book of Revelations: "**I am** the alpha and **I am** the omega. The beginning and the end." He didn't say I *was* the alpha and I *will be* the omega because He is present in our past and our future.

Wherever our lives take us, we need not fear because God is already there. I can rest because the great **I am** is beside me wherever **I am**! And He's beside you too.

# ENEMIES & STAMPS

## ROMANS 12:17-21

*P*ostage stamps **cost** a lot. Funny thing, loving our enemies **costs** a lot too. We have to **invest** in forgiveness. And put aside the **wealth** of anger we feel. We **foreclose** on any resentment. We **subtract** harsh words. We look beyond the person's **debt** of wrongs. We **credit** them as one of God's children. We **spend** time to express that love. And finally we **count** our blessings. Loving our enemies **costs** us plenty, much more than **pocket change** to **change** our attitudes.

As Christians we are called to look beyond the **balance sheet** and what we can **profit** and what we have **lost**. God asks us to **take inventory** of the **price** Jesus **paid** for us. God **credits** us **depositing** grace upon grace so that our **account** is never **bankrupt**. Out of these great **riches** we are to **repay** evil with good. Is there an enemy's **bad debt** you can **negate** today?

# WHY IS THE SKY BLUE?

## 1 CORINTHIANS 12:12-14

*a*s I struggled to unbuckle my son from his impossible car seat, my daughter tugged on my shorts nearly pulling them down to my knees. She wanted an answer to her pressing question, "Why is the sky blue, Momma?" Exasperated I offered, "I think blue is God's favorite color." Honestly, I had forgotten why the sky was blue. (I had also forgotten my grocery list on the kitchen counter.) Later I learned online that the blue color of the sky and ocean result from the scattering of sunlight by particles. [1]

This made me think. Just as particles scatter sunlight to color the sky and ocean, we each are called to scatter the light of Christ to "color" the face of the earth. Though one glass of water lacks color, when poured into the lake it appears blue. Together we can make a difference coloring the world with kindness!

# CANTALOUPES AND ENVELOPES JOIN OKRA AND OPRAH

MATTHEW 6:7-13

*G*od is great. God is good. Let us thank Him for our food.

An ordinary prayer can be shared over ordinary food but there's something extra-ordinary about family meal time. No matter what happens during our *unpredictable* day, what happens *predictably* around our table makes life feel lighter. We fill our tummies with food and our souls with encouragement. Last night we giggled as my son nibbled on fresh cantaloupe after he bounced and announced, "I love fresh 'envelope!'" And we still call okra (the vegetable) Oprah (the philanthropist) because my daughter insists that's its name.

We talk about our hopes and our dreams, our disappointments and our fears. Sharing lifts us up and lets us know we are never alone. When you say an ordinary blessing over ordinary food, what extra-ordinary memories might become part of your family's perfectly imperfect story?

# LEPROSY AND LONELINESS

## LUKE 12:11-19

$\mathcal{M}$ other Teresa insisted, "the biggest disease today is not leprosy...but rather the feeling of being unwanted, uncared for and deserted by everybody." We may not be destitute and dying in the slums of Calcutta, but we each can relate to Mother Teresa's notion. While we likely have not experienced leprosy, we each have experienced loneliness.

Loneliness and depression have more than just the same number of syllables in common. They often live together like lepers, quarantined as unwanted neighbors.

Loneliness and depression rob us of joy, making us the "poorest of the poor." But like Mother Teresa, who loved the lost and the lonely, we can too. Love can be the antidote to loneliness. God offered it unconditionally for our healing and He wants us to share His love unashamedly. Like Mother Teresa we can leave a lasting legacy of love.

# KISSES FOR BABY JESUS

## MARK 10:13-16

When out for a walk my toddler spotted a life-size plastic manger scene. You would have thought she was Christopher Columbus pointing out land. "Look Mommy, dat's BABY JESUS!" Alyssa bounded across our neighbor's lawn to rock Him in her arms, giving Him hugs and kisses. I stood frozen on the sidewalk wondering if anyone was watching her trespass.

Then it hit me. How often am I too embarrassed to show my love for Jesus because of what others might think? There are times I don't speak up or stand up and share like I should.

Jesus said: "Let the children come to me. Don't stop them! For the Kingdom of Heaven belongs to those like them." Today my toddler taught us how to run unashamedly to Jesus!

# B.F.F. & B.F.G.

## 1 CORINTHIANS 13:1-10

*B*.F.G. was listed among those most admired by the Gallup poll sixty-one times! He received the Presidential Medal of Freedom and met with every president from Harry Truman to Barack Obama.

He even received a star on the Hollywood Walk of Fame and was knighted by Queen Elizabeth. He wrote thirty-three books and traveled to 185 countries speaking to over 215 million people, which is almost half of the world's population. Closer to home, he was the second president of the University of Northwestern, starting the first Northwestern Media radio station.

His momma called him William Franklyn but we knew him as (drum roll) Billy Graham! Billy was admired because he resembled Jesus. He is remembered for sharing the love of Jesus, his B.F.F. Who do you most resemble and how will people remember you?

# WELL DONE-WELL SAID

## MATTHEW 25:14-18

*B*enjamin Franklin believed, "Well done is better than well said." My dad agreed, insisting, "talk is cheap." He taught me to "put one foot in front of the other every day."

Sometimes I don't feel like I'm making much progress. But together with Jesus by our side, if you and I do our best and love others despite setbacks, we can look back and see how far we've come.

Then at the end of our lives, it will be wonderful to hear our Father say: "Well **done** my good and faithful servant. You've been faithful in handling this small amount so now I will give you many more responsibilities. Let's celebrate together."

Heaven can't be described with black ink that forms words on a white page. We are promised by Jesus Himself that no eye has seen and no ear has heard what God has prepared for us. That's exciting!

# GOD'S FAVORITE GIFT

ROMANS 8:14-17

"What you are is God's gift to you. What you make of yourself is your gift to God." Those eighteen words were on a plaque my high school coach, Ms. Roxanne, gave me when I was eighteen.

Now I'm twice that old and those eighteen words have stuck with me. Although this isn't a direct quote from the Bible, it is based on many of Jesus' parables.

As a parent now myself, I realize that the very best gift we could ever give God is our love. Think about it in terms of your own children. You don't love them based on *what* they have become. Whether they are a psychiatrist or a secretary, a street sweeper or a substitute teacher, you love them because of *who* they are. They are your child. Through Jesus we are adopted into God's family and He loves us because we are His children.

# BLOW DRYERS N' CAR WASHES

PSALM 19:1-6

*C*ar washes and blow dryers are nothing too exciting for us, but they are riveting for my kiddos. My preschooler's favorite outing this month is to drive through the car wash. Sitting on my lap behind the steering wheel, her giggles boomerang off the windows as they are bombarded with water. "I'm not ascared," she bounces and announces.

My son is equally blown away by my blow dryer. He watches intensely as I dry my hair. His eyes are glued first to me, then to my hair waving wildly and then to the dryer itself. He loves to feel the warm air fly past his face. While simple activities like driving through a car wash or drying your hair may not seem noteworthy, a sunrise or sunset is a wonder-worthy moment that God provides every day. How long has it been since you've paused to watch how exquisitely He ushers in the morning and how magnificently He brings your day's journey to a close?

# M & M'S®

LUKE 10:38-42

oday God encouraged me with M & M's. Though I love the chocolate M & M® candies, God encouraged me with the M & M sisters-Mary and Martha-from the Bible. In three verses, we encounter these two sisters. One was short-tempered, short on help and short on time. Martha was worried and upset over the details of dinner.

I can be like Martha, so I am comforted to know that Jesus says there's only one thing worth being concerned about and that's Him. Mary chose the best...to rest with Jesus.

Truly, the devil's in the details when the details distract us from Jesus. No matter how busy your day, keep your thoughts focused on Jesus so you're not "worried and distracted." That's the sweet message of the colorful M & M sisters!

# THE MOON AND THE SON

MATTHEW 25:34-40

 *U*nlike the sun, the moon produces no light. Rather it reflects the sun's light. And just as the moon reflects the sun's light, we are called to reflect the Son's light. The more we know the Son, the more we are filled with His Light, becoming His lights to the world.

What are some ways we can "light up the world"? We're told to feed the hungry, give drink to the thirsty, invite a stranger home, give clothes to the needy and visit the sick and imprisoned. While few of us have actually been in a prison, we all have felt imprisoned by something. Fear. Loneliness. Addictions. Dead-end jobs or declining health.

When we bring hope and comfort to those who are prisoners to circumstances, we're sharing Christ's light. Can you think of one way today that you can be like the moon and reflect the Son's light, brightening someone's darkness?

# SHINY PENNIES & SHINING EXAMPLES

HEBREWS 6:18-20

When you were young, did someone older encourage you? And what do you most remember about them? Though I don't remember her name, I do remember her orthopedic stockings, her smiling eyes and her kind touch. She was the plump volunteer with a soft heart who sat on a hard folding chair collecting our lunch money.

Back then I thought she was there just to collect shiny pennies for her grandson. Now I understand that she was called to give priceless encouragement. It didn't matter if you misspelled vacuum in the spelling bee, kicked the ball out of bounds twice at recess and forgot your lunch money. Her kindness made your day better. Though hot lunches nourished me for an afternoon, her example of love has nourished my soul for many seasons. Like me, every time you see a shiny penny might you be inspired by her shining example to encourage others?

# FLASHLIGHT AND FEARS

PSALM 46:1-11

My preschooler just learned how to lock doors and she practiced her big-girl talent with one flaw. She locked herself inside the dark bathroom leaving her Godmother outside.

Alyssa had her piece of pizza in one hand and her flashlight in the other. Sharon pleaded with her to lay down her flashlight and use both hands to turn the knob and pop the lock. But Alyssa was too afraid to let go of her flashlight. Her pizza hand was too greasy to grip the knob.

Sometimes we're a lot like Alyssa. We cling to what **we** know best, instead of trusting the **One** who knows best. Psalm 46 promises: "God is our refuge and strength, an ever-present help in trouble. Therefore we will not fear." Will you lay down your fears and let Him into the darkest, locked rooms of your heart?

# HIDDEN TREASURES

## MATTHEW 13:44-46

*A*fter I saw King Tut's hidden treasures on exhibit in Chicago, I wanted to be an archeologist. At nine hidden treasures of any kind were exciting.

Recently I cleaned under the couch cushions and my toddler was thrilled finding hidden treasures. There were pennies, popcorn and puzzle pieces. We found Mr. Potato Head's long lost ear and Baby Heart Beat's stethoscope. Alyssa's eyes were as big as Oreos finding these hidden treasures. The Bible tells us that: "The Kingdom of Heaven is like a treasure that a man discovered hidden in a field. In his excitement, he hid it again and sold everything he owned to get enough money to buy the field." Sometimes we are hum-ho about our faith, but a verse like this makes my heart beat a bit faster reminding me that heaven will be better than any hidden treasure here on earth.

# A HUNGRY TODDLER

## MATTHEW 11:28-30

*A*t four in the morning, our four-year-old carried the chair from her tea table to our bedroom so she could reach the light switch. With one flip she gave new meaning to the phrase, "Let there be light!" Dave shot straight up in bed and Alyssa greeted him with a cheery request, "I hungry. I need pantakes."

Are you ever hungry for more than the ordinary? I am. On days I feel empty I'm comforted by Jesus who said: "Come to me, all of you who are weary and carry heavy burdens, and I will give you rest. Take my yoke upon you. Let me teach you, because I am humble and gentle in heart, and you will find rest for your souls." Next time you find yourself awake in the wee hours of the morning, whether by a hungry toddler or a wearisome worry, switch on the light to read God's Word. There you can find much needed rest for your soul!

# PEOPLE PLEASERS AND
# POSTUREPEDICS®

## GALATIANS 1:10

*B*eing a people pleaser is a personal weakness. I don't like to disappoint anyone. When I think others are upset with me, I lose sleep. Yet I married a man who hasn't lost any sleep because he's worried about what others think.

I can learn from my hubby and from Paul who writes, "I'm not trying to win the approval of people, but of God. If pleasing people were my goal, I would not be Christ's servant."

Knowing that we only need to please Christ simplifies our days. It has also prompted me to ask myself this question to calm my concern: "When I stand before God's throne, will this matter?" If not, then I remind myself that it's just a speed bump in the road of life. This practical perspective helps me sleep better than any Posturepedic®!

# DUST OF COMPARISON

## HEBREWS 12:1-3

We've all done it. We let comparison creep into our thoughts like dust creeps into our homes. Dust does no one any good. Practically speaking, how do we clean the dust of comparison out of our minds? The Bible tells us to, "Strip off everything that slows us down. And let us run with endurance the race God has set before us. We do this by keeping our eyes on Jesus, the champion who initiates and perfects our faith."

In Biblical times runners would quite literally strip down to their birthday suits so that they could sprint without the extra weight of clothing. While I wouldn't want to run that way, I certainly could lose the emotional burden of comparison. Christ is our dust-free, shining example. He will help us run the race perfecting our faith. Dust has no place in our homes just as comparison has no place in our minds.

# PEZ®

## PSALM 51:10-19

*A*s a kid Pez® candy dispensers were such fun. My daughter loves the dispenser even more than the candy. She pretends the Pez® are pills, calling them "mouth medicine."

Sometimes I need more than mouth medicine. What comes out of the mouth of a Pez® dispenser is sugary. What comes out of my mouth isn't always so sweet. The Bible tells me that what comes out of my mouth is a reflection of what's inside of my heart.

If I want my words to change, I need my heart to change. Like King David I need God to "create in me a clean heart." Then I can live the truth of Proverbs which says: "Kind words are like honey-sweet to the soul and healthy for the body." While my daughter doesn't need Pez® candies, we each need sweet words for our souls. Let's encourage one another today.

# INVISIBLE INK

## ROMANS 1:20

*I*nvisible ink markers are nerdy fun! With one end you write a top-secret message. Then with the other end, you scribble over the letters making the invisible message suddenly visible. While invisible markers are great for kids, God reveals invisible truths through His creation. In Romans 1:20 we learn: "For ever since the world was created, people have seen the earth and sky. Through everything God made, they can clearly see his invisible qualities."

Sometimes I envision setbacks as God's invisible hand reaching through time to spark patience. I see a sister's faith through her good works. Sometimes I discover peace hidden in sorrows. You might find His joy nestled in the corners of a child's question or feel forgiveness in a hug. You could experience His gentleness in the kiss of a kiddo. When you reach out to others, you are the visible hand of our invisible God.

# POSITIVE PETALS

## PHILIPPIANS 4:8-9

*R*oses are the most popular flower given to express love. When my husband and I were dating we were poor paying off college debt. Having both been raised in frugal families, we appreciated small splurges. Miniature roses were a splurge. At a gas-station-turned-flower-shop, David would buy me a dozen miniature roses for $9.99. Even today when I receive roses from him, not only is each petal a reminder of his love, but it's a reminder to focus daily on *the positives...the petals.*

Along with petals, roses have thorns. Likewise, spouses have thorns or imperfections. But when we see a rose, we don't concentrate on its thorns. In Philippians 4 we're told: "Think about things that are excellent and worthy of praise and the God of peace will be with you." So today might you choose to be an instrument of peace and to see the fragrant good in people rather than focus on their thorny shortcomings?

# FROZEN

PHILIPPIANS 4:10-14

*A*lthough everything is frozen outside, I'm warm and toasty inside having just watched the Disney animated movie *Frozen* with my daughter. I love the story of Anna-the fearless princess-who journeys to find Elsa, her sister, who accidentally froze the kingdom.

As I sit with a mug of cocoa, I realize feeling frozen or stuck by overwhelming circumstances is part of everyone's story. I often want God to magically un-thaw my kingdom, like Princess Elsa in *Frozen,* but He doesn't. On a very practical level, when I'm frozen I've found it's useful to write down what I need to accomplish. I slice an overwhelming job into fork-sized chunks of digestible work. Then when I accomplish each small task, I can cross it off with a big black marker, which is so satisfying. With God we don't need to stay frozen. What can He help you accomplish today?

# SWIMMING LESSONS AND LIFE

PSALM 23:1-6

*G*rowing up swimming lessons were so scary. I still remember kids with blue lips shivering toward me as I stood like an ice cube frozen to the pavement. I was as cold as the banana split my Mom had promised me if I did well. And I was ready to split, heading straight for the nearest exit, which happened to be the boy's locker room.

Becoming a parent and making my kids take swimming lessons has given me a new perspective. The more years I walk with my heavenly Father, the more I know He walks right beside me through the "valley of the shadow of death." Sometimes the valley looks like a BIG pool to a little girl.

Sometimes the valley looks like a demotion, a divorce or even a death. Whatever trials you face today, know that God is swimming right beside you cheering you on. Our King's rewards will far exceed Dairy Queen's banana split!

# STUCK IN A SNOW GLOBE

JOHN 1:1-12

*a*s kids we each had our favorite Christmas traditions and decorations. My three-year-old is intrigued by our snow globe that plays music. She squeals as the snow swirls around the baby's manger, pointing out, "Dat's baby Jesus stuck in there with His Mommy and His Daddy to-o-o-o!"

Do you ever feel trapped like a plastic figure in a snow globe? Perhaps you feel stuck in a belittling job, a big mortgage or bad decisions. I think Jesus can relate. Before He came to this earth and donned a human body, He was not limited by space and time. Then the Creator of the universe became bound by a body.

During this Christmas season, we celebrate the coming of our Savior. When the snows of this life are swirling, know that just as my daughter holds the snow globe in her hands, Jesus holds you in His hands. Like my daughter, He doesn't take His eyes off of you. You bring Him joy!

# CORN ON THE COB

1 TIMOTHY 6:6-12

*W*ould you rather have a piece of corn on the cob that still has the strings from the husk or a piece that had no strings but no corn? My daughter delights in finding strings. It's a challenge her little fingers can't pass up. And my son loves to suck on the bare cob. Add some butter and he kicks his legs and bounces in his highchair.

Barefoot on the back porch after dinner, I remember sucking butter from the bare cob as a kid. But then I grew up and became too dignified for such behavior.

As adults it's so easy to look at other people's "corn" and no longer be content with just our "cob." Jesus knew this and tells us that we need to be humble like children and welcome wonder. No matter how tired He was, Jesus always welcomed children. No matter how old we are, we are still His children and He always welcomes us.

# TASTE BUDS

## 1 CORINTHIANS 10:31-33

God created us with over 10,000 discerning taste buds. That makes the area on our tongue prime real estate. Of all my senses I **most** delight in my sense of taste, yet I need it the **least**. Make no mistake, I would still feel hungry and I would still eat, just as I feel thirsty and still drink water though it has no taste.

God did not **need** to give you and me the ability to taste. We could function fine without ever savoring a thing. Honestly, we wouldn't know what we were missing. But I believe God **wants** to gift us with the sense of taste so we can experience joy.

Good gifts point us to our good gift Giver. Whatever we eat or drink we are to do it for the glory of God. I'm convinced that the pleasure we experience through food allows us to experience an appetizer of the delight to come in heaven. There we will feast with God. Diets don't exist in heaven.

# SOULMATES OR HELPMATES?

## GENESIS 2:18

Having a "soulmate" sounds so perfectly dreamy. Being a "helpmate"...not so much. Today we talk a lot about finding our soulmate, but the Bible never does. Our souls are eternal and can only be truly satisfied by God. Another person at some point will disappoint.

Marriage exists only on earth "until death do us part." In heaven, like the angels, we won't be married. So while the Bible never talks about soulmates, it does talk about being a helpmate.

Here on Earth we don't have to be married to help others. Ephesians 2:20 reminds us, "for we are his workmanship, created in Christ Jesus for good works, which God prepared beforehand, that we should walk in them." In giving ourselves away, we become complete...whole and holy. There is a holiness to helpfulness.

# A FANCY WORD

## EPHESIANS 2:8-9

*I*'ve heard it said that religion will keep more people from heaven than anything else. If acting religious **outwardly** becomes more important than knowing Christ **inwardly**, this might be true. The Bible tells us that no one can ever be made right with God by doing what the law commands. The law simply shows us how sinful we are and how badly we need grace.

By grace we are saved through faith, not by works. Adding legal requirements to earn salvation is called "legalism." My dad would call legalism a fancy word. He would say it means we're trying to work our way into heaven.

Salvation is a gift from Jesus our Savior. When we give a gift, we don't ask the receiver to pay us back. Grace is a gift. Nothing we do can earn it and nothing we do can lose it.

# THE EXTRA MILE

## MATTHEW 5:38-42

Going the "extra mile." It feels so good when someone does it for us. Jesus said: "If a soldier demands that you carry his gear for one mile, carry it two miles." Not only was this physically difficult, it was demeaning. Yet Jesus encourages us to carry loads twice the distance.

Today instead of carrying a soldier's burdensome gear, we may be asked to listen to ease another's emotional burden. We may be asked to carry a colleague's workload while they're on maternity leave.

We may be asked to help carry a friend through the loss of a loved one, a divorce or an illness. Maybe we will be asked to help care for aging parents or ease the financial burden of a relative. If so, Jesus encourages us to "go the extra mile."

## TONGUE TWISTERS

"Peter Piper, pick up your peppers!" My daughter doesn't have this twister memorized perfectly, but she perfectly imitates me as she shakes her finger reminding her brother to pick up his toys.

She inspired me to come up with my own tongue twister. Wanna hear it? **Potent, powerful promises provide a perfect paradox.** When we're faced with trouble God promises: "My power works best in your weakness." This is a paradox and it's also a powerful promise perfect for those times we need uplifted.

Relying on God when we feel like we are at the end of our rope is so wise. Psalm 46 tells us that, "God is our refuge and strength, an ever-present help in trouble." So call out then reach out for help so that in your weakness you are stronger than ever.

# PLAQUE AND PRIDE

## PROVERBS 16:18

My dental hygienist flashes me a smile & hangs a saliva straw over my lip. As she scrapes hardened plaque from my teeth, I realize how much plaque and pride have in common.

Before my appointment I had read Proverbs 16: "First pride, then the crash—the bigger the ego, the harder the fall." Self-pride is arrogance and can erode our life much like plaque can erode our teeth.

But is all pride bad? Surely we can be proud of our children or spouse for a job well done. When accomplishments bring God glory, it's good. But when we internalize our accomplishments and claim the glory for ourselves, it's bad.

So while brushing your teeth tonight, be reminded to brush pride from your ego by giving God all the glory for all your accomplishments.

# TWO STICKS OF WARM BUTTER

## PSALM 37:11

ike two sticks of warm butter, meek and weak seem to melt together in our minds. We associate meekness with weakness. Not many folks would describe themselves as meek on a job interview or a first date. But God treasures meekness as a spiritual quality. It is humility of heart.

Of all the men on the face of the Earth, Moses was said to be the meekest. Jesus describes Himself as "meek and lowly in heart." And He turns our thinking upside down and inside out when He tells us that, "those who are meek are blessed and will inherit the earth." So while the world may associate meekness with weakness, we know that meekness is powerful.

Meekness mirrors Christ our King. It requires great restraint to submit to others in humility and gentleness. So of all the adjectives that you could use to describe yourself, being meek is one of the most majestic.

# OUR WASHER'S SPIN CYCLE

PSALM 8:1-9

Sometimes our daily routine feels like we're caught in our washer's spin cycle and we feel pulled more directions than a bra that has escaped the lingerie bag.

When our laundry pile resembles *Mt. Everest*, we feel like we can *never rest*. But when we turn to scripture and slow down, God shows up. And when we kneel down, He lifts us up. We can find more than lost socks in the dryer when we are paired with God through prayer. And when we cling to His truths, like socks to a sweater, life becomes sweeter.

Between loads of laundry to be done and lullabies to be sung, we may see majestic moments folded between mundane moments. Then we can say like the psalmist, "O Lord, our Lord, how majestic is your name in all the earth! You have set your glory above the heavens. Out of the mouth of babies and infants you have established strength."

# SIDE STITCH AND SHIN SPLINTS

## ISAIAH 40:29-31

While we're all part of the human race, we don't need to succumb to the rat race! Jesus understands our need for rest which is why He and His Father led by example. After creating the universe, they rested from work on the seventh day. While on earth Jesus also rested on the Sabbath.

When my spirit is hurried and harried, I'm more prone to be worried and weary. For me hurry and worry go together like side stitch and shin splints. Both result from running too hard for too long. But our God "gives power to the weak and strength to the powerless. Even youths will become weak and tired, and young men will fall in exhaustion, but those who trust in the Lord will find new strength. They will soar high on wings like eagles. They will run and not grow weary. They will walk and not faint." So let's set aside the rat race and rest with Jesus-Our Prince of Peace.

# TYLENOL® AND TRUTH

## LUKE 16:10

ylenol® and truth have more in common than you might initially think. Just as the little white tablets of Tylenol® are common and seem harmless, the little white lies we tell are common and seem harmless. Though you and I differentiate levels or degrees of lies, scripture does not. Darkness cannot exist in the presence of Light. Lies cannot exist in the presence of Truth.

The issue at hand is larger. Jesus explains that, "If we are faithful in little things, we will also be faithful in big things. But if we are dishonest in little things, we won't be honest with greater responsibilities." This prompts me to ask myself if I'm truthful in matters that may seem insignificant.

To God the small things matter. Words, like Tylenol®, can be used to heal or to harm. So together let's use our words so that they are always uplifting!

# FAITH AND POPCORN

## LUKE 6:38

*F*resh popcorn with warm butter smells so good! While waiting for a batch to pop, I realized how much a kernel has in common with faith. Heat transforms each kernel into something that's nourishing and fills our tummies. Likewise, hot trials transform our faith into something that is nourishing and fills our souls.

The Bible tells us that faith without works is of little value to anyone. Likewise, a bowl of unpopped kernels is of little value to a hungry snacker.

Living out our faith, we're called by Jesus to kind deeds like feeding the hungry. I want my good deeds to pop the lid off others' expectations. Like an overflowing bowl of popcorn, I want my kindness to overflow and feed those around me. Offering a listening ear and a kind word is so simple yet so scrumptious to the starving soul.

## LOVE, HEARTS & TWO SHEPHERD'S STAFFS

### ISAIAH 40:11

*I*'m no artist but even I can draw a heart. It looks like two shepherds' staffs joined together on each end. The shepherd staff reminds us that Jesus is our Good Shepherd.

While a heart is easy to draw, it teaches us a difficult lesson about love. Just as a shepherd uses a staff to draw sheep back, sometimes God pulls us back to keep us safe. It doesn't always feel good to be pulled back.

Sometimes putting our children first pulls us out of the running for a promotion at work. I've experienced this. Other times putting our husband's needs first means pulling back on our plans to start a ministry. This too was my reality. But sometimes the Good Shepherd sees things that we don't see. Know that you can lean on God, just as a shepherd leans on his staff.

# YOUR MIND~GOD'S HANDS

## ISAIAH 41:10

*W*hatever is **on** your mind is **in** God's hands. God cares about our cares. The Bible tells us to cast our cares on Him because He cares for us. One minute I give God my worries and the next minute I'm grabbing them back. Know the feeling? At those times I open my Bible to verses about peace like Isaiah 26:3: "You will keep in perfect peace all who trust in you, all whose thoughts are fixed on you!"

Fixing my thoughts on God rather than trying to fix the person I'm mad at is hard. But God comforts us saying, "Don't be afraid for I am with you. Don't be discouraged for I am your God. I will strengthen you and help you. I will hold you up with my victorious right hand." So when your mind starts to ruminate on worrisome "what ifs" remember whatever is **on** your mind is **in** God's hands! We don't know what the future holds, but we know Who holds the future.

# HOW MUCH YOU CARE

## ROMANS 2:1-4

*T*eddy Roosevelt said, "No one cares how much you know, until they know how much you care."[1] No one wants to be around a know-it-all. A person wrapped up in themselves makes a very small package. Having them present is no present. But everyone wants to be around someone who is kind. Kindness is attractive and attracts others. Perhaps that's because when we're kind, we look like Christ.

The Bible tells us that God's kindness leads us and others to repentance. So if we are wanting to help others find Christ and don't know where to start, let's start with kindness.

Together we can make a difference. In 2020 Covid was contagious. Let's make kindness contagious all decade long! After all, no one cares how much you know, until they know how much you care!

# QUARREL-PAST-PRESENT

## PROVERBS 20:3

*W*inston Churchill once said: "If we open a quarrel between the past and the present, we will find that we have lost the future." The Bible tells us: "Avoiding a fight is a mark of honor; only fools insist on quarreling." Being "quick to listen, slow to speak and slow to anger" is hard because it feels so good to get the last word.

But Jesus tells us: "Blessed are the peacemakers, for they shall be called the children of God." It's only with our Father's help that we can "listen fast and get angry last." Leaving the last word unspoken is a spiritual discipline when the last word only fuels the fire.

Saying we're sorry when we've hurt others with our words requires humility of heart. This meekness is treasured by God. So here's to honoring our Father by settling our quarrels before the sun sets on our anger and we lose sleep.

# DO YOU "DO WINDOWS?"

MATTHEW 28:16-20

*D*o you "do windows?" I don't...at least not very often. My toddler loves to clean windows, or maybe I should more correctly share, she loves to spray. It doesn't matter if it's Windex® or water.

As I watch her I wonder if we as Christians could be called to "do windows?" To clean off whatever clouds us from seeing God's wonder and grace in our lives and share that grace.

Based on hundreds of scriptures in the New Testament alone, I believe that God calls each of us. Though we are not all called to be pastors **in** a church, He does call us to be ministers of love **to** the church and to those outside the churches.

Can you see what God would want you to accomplish today or are the windows of your reality smeared with the handprints of the world? I need to daily clean the window of **my** will off so I can clearly see **His** will.

# BRAIN FREEZE

## EXODUS 34:9

*a*n ice cream brain freeze hurts. It's our brain's way to say it doesn't like change. The drop in temperature from the ice cream causes the blood vessels in our throat to constrict from the cold. When these vessels warm up, they open up allowing blood to rush in causing pain.[1]

Like my brain, I don't like cold changes especially when it comes to my children giving me the cold shoulder. I think our Father understands this pain well. Just like our kids, Adam and Eve didn't appreciate the perfect home He created for them. Then His chosen people rejected Him again and again even though He provided for their every need.

I'm no different. Some days I am unappreciative and too busy to make time for Him. Our Father is crazy about us just like we're crazy about our kids. God understands that both kids and ice cream can bring pain.

# NO DIET

## DEUTERONOMY 8:1-5

My preschooler loves Juicy Fruit® but is disappointed when she swallows a stick. She thinks all gum is edible. This reminds me of the edible gum or manna God gave to His people when they wandered in the desert. This manna was like gummy bread, but it was so much more. It was a foretaste of the Bread of Life. Today Jesus is our manna sent from heaven. Just as manna needed to be collected every morning before the sun came out and melted it, we need the Living Bread of Jesus every morning before our courage is melted by hot trials. Manna couldn't be stored for the next day or it "bred worms and stank." Every day each person was to gather and eat the equivalent of three quarts. That's twelve cups. This is God's way of saying that we are not to skip our spiritual meals. He doesn't want us to be hungry and vulnerable. You gotta love His "no diet" approach to our spiritual food.

# A PRODIGAL OR A PRODIGY?

LUKE 15:11-32

*B*eing a loving parent is hard. This morning I was reading *The Parable of the Prodigal Son* about the boy who demanded his inheritance early which was in effect saying to his dad, "you're dead to me." Bringing shame to his family he ditched his dad. When he was broke and starving, he remembered his home. Truly sorry, he remembered he was loved.

Like the father in the story who watched for his son, God watches and waits for us. You may have grown up, grown busy or grown distant, but always know that your heavenly Father doesn't care where you've been or what you've wasted, He's just glad when you come home.

Whether you're a prodigy or a prodigal or someone in between like me, you're God's child and He wants you to come home when you hunger. You might think you're *ordinary*, but He thinks you're *extraordinary*!

# WONDER WOMEN

## DEUTERONOMY 31:6

*A*s women we often feel like we need to be Wonder Women with superhuman powers to accomplish all our tasks to be a good Christian, wife, mother, daughter, friend and coworker. But do we?

Though we don't have Wonder Woman's golden lasso of truth, we do have His Word which is Truth. And while we don't have bracelets that deflect bullets, we do have Christ who goes before us.

When we crave extraordinary God-moments in the ordinary, we hunger for God's wonder. And that makes us Wonder Women.

So in the end we don't need to strive to be a superhuman Marvel® hero because we have a superhuman marvelous Hero and Savior! So here's to being Wonder Women (and Wonder Men) who rock this world!

# ZIPPERS

## GENESIS 2:24

My preschooler just learned how to work zippers. Recently we were at the Department of Motor Vehicles. As I was paying the clerk while holding my nine-month-old, Alyssa was practicing her new skills with my zipper. Thanks to a single button, my skirt didn't fall to my ankles giving those in line behind me something to talk about.

This near mishap got me thinking about how much zippers have in common with marriage. The pull on a zipper brings two pieces of material together, just as God through marriage brings two people together. We read in Genesis that, "man leaves his father and mother and is united to his wife, and they become one flesh." Just as my zipper needs the pull to keep it together, my hubby and I need God to pull us together. With God, all things are possible!

# THE TEACHING STEPS

## PSALM 104:1-5

*I*srael is amazing to visit. While in the Holy Land, of all my steps the most amazing were those taken on the Temple's Teaching Steps in Jerusalem. Jesus once walked and taught on these steps. What engaged me most was the stairs' unique design. Every step varied in height, depth and width. Climbing them was difficult. With each being different, there was "cause to pause." I needed to step purposefully...to evaluate my next step forward so I didn't miscalculate and misstep. This made me alert to my surroundings. The steps were designed this way to encourage sojourners to slow down...to make and take each step with purpose.

Even today God can use difficulties to give us "cause to pause," prompting us to be purposeful. What would our life look like if every pause was pregnant with expectation and every step carried us closer to God's presence?

# MAC N' CHEESE AND SKINNED KNEES

## JEREMIAH 31:34

*M*ac n' cheese and skinned knees. Both are a part of childhood. As parents we wipe alligator tears from our kiddo's eyes and wish we could take away the sting that asphalt brings. Though the wound isn't deep, God has a deep lesson to teach us from the simplest of cuts.

God wants us to clean out the dirt and give Him the hurt. Wounds must be cleaned of debris to heal. He asks us to clean bitterness from our emotional wounds and forgive others as He forgives us.

Forgiveness is salve to our souls. So say it out loud. Father, I forgive _____ for hurting me. Please take the hurt, heal my heart and make me healthy and whole in Jesus' name. Amen.

# NOSE AND HAIR

## LUKE 12:1-7

*B*oth your nose and your hair lengthen with time. It's a medical fact your nose lengthens each decade. It's a medical myth, however, that the more often you trim your hair the faster it will grow. Because hair itself is dead, it never *grows*; however, the hair follicle produces more hair thus hair *lengthens*. Jesus knew this and explains: "The very hairs on your head are all numbered." As a child, I remember being fascinated that God knew how many hairs I had both before and after brushing. I would yank one out occasionally just to make sure He was paying attention. As adults we might ask ourselves why Jesus talks about our dead hair. I think He wants us to comprehend how completely He loves us. This perfect love fills us, casting out all fear. So the next time you brush your hair and see all the hair left in your brush, smile knowing you are cherished!

# SALES, SOFT SOIL & SHRUBS

## MARK 4:1-20

Clearance sales make me smile. Recently I snagged beautiful evergreens on clearance for five dollars each. Needing to replace shrubs around our home, what I expected to cost hundreds cost me pennies on the dollar. Even my hubby was excited about this sale. And because it had been such a wet summer, the earth was soft, making them easy to plant.

As I dug a hole in the ground, God reminded me of the importance of the soil of my heart. My heart is soft when it is saturated with living water. There the seed of God's Word can take root and grow evergreen with faith, hope and love. More than bargain bushes we buy for a few bucks, faith, hope and love are the enduring landscape of the Christian life.

# THE LITTLE ENGINE THAT COULD

## PHILIPPIANS 4:4-13

*W*e all remember the wonder-filled story of *The Little Engine That Could*. On her way to deliver a cargo of magical toys, Georgia, the engine, suddenly breaks down. Pete, the powerful freight engine, and Farnsworth, the shiny passenger engine, refuse to help. Rusty old Jebediah is just too worn out, but a little switch engine named Tillie thinks she can do it.

Today when I read this classic to my daughter, I thought of Jesus who tells us: "The things which are impossible with men are possible with God." Based on this promise, we can do more than say, "I think I can. I think I can. I think I can." We can live out the truth, "In Christ we can. In Christ we can. In Christ we can." What can you do powered by Jesus today?

# PRETTY OR PETTY?

## 1 CORINTHIANS 13:4-6

*I* recently read: You are only as pretty as you treat people. We've all experienced petty people when what we really needed was someone who was patient and kind.

- We need friends who aren't jealous, proud, demanding or rude.
- We need spouses who aren't irritable and don't keep a list of all the ways they've been wronged.
- We need coworkers who believe in us, never give up on us and hope the best for us.

Perhaps that's why the Bible puts much more emphasis on how we "love" than how we "look." Might we make it our goal to be "lovely," because petty people are not pretty?

# GINORMOUS GIANTS

## 1 SAMUEL 17:45-51

hen some people see a giant they say, "He is so big!" while others say, "He is so big, I can't miss!" Giants aren't just named Goliath and live in the land of Gath. No. Giants visit our homes in all shapes and sizes.

Sometimes our Goliath is a difficult boss or a bad habit. Sometimes our giant is a mountain of debt. Maybe it is a diabetes diagnosis or a depressing divorce. Whatever your giant, know that, like David, you can proclaim, "You come against me with sword and spear..., but I come against you in the name of the LORD Almighty...This day the LORD will hand you over to me, and I'll strike you down and cut off your head."

In God's hands your sling and stone is better than any sword or spear. Your giant may be BIG, but with God, you can't miss. What will you say to your giant today?

# REFINE NOT DEFINE

## JEREMIAH 29:11

*H*ardships don't **define** us, they **refine** us. Failures don't define you. In God's hands, they refine you. Whatever hard trial you're going through right now, know that God will work all things together for your good.

You may have been flunked by a teacher, fired by a boss, forgotten by a friend or forsaken by a spouse, but God says you are Favored, Forgiven, Freed and Filled with the Spirit. Through Faith you are saved to Fellowship with Him Forever.

Believe God when He says in Jeremiah 29:11: "'For I know the plans I have for you,' declares the Lord, 'plans to prosper you and not to harm you, plans to give you hope and a future.'" Failures don't define you. Rather God uses them like a Master Artisan to refine you so you shine brilliantly like a diamond.

# SMALL THINGS WITH GREAT LOVE

## MATTHEW 25:40

Mother Teresa always said, "In this life we cannot always do great things. But we can do small things with great love."[1] My own mother always said, "Do one good deed every day." So often we think we will reach out to others when life slows down…when we get a better job…when we retire. But often when we arrive at one success milestone, we face other challenges. Mother Teresa shared, "I am not called to be successful, but to be faithful." This small-statured woman won many big awards like the Nobel Peace Prize, but she is remembered most because of her small acts of great kindness.

The key to leaving a legacy isn't necessarily doing large things but doing "small things with great love." Loving my husband, children and neighbors well will be my greatest legacy, not the initials after my name or the diploma that hangs on my wall. What will your legacy be?

# WHITE SPACE & FREE TIME

## EXODUS 20:8-11

*B*elieve it or not, the white lines that dash and divide our roadways are as long as our cars. Yet the faster we go, the shorter they seem. Today as I sped down the highway, it struck me that these white lines are like "white space" in our lives. The faster we go, the less "white space" we see. White space is the new term for free time or rest. But the idea of rest is not new.

Rest is so important, it made God's top ten list. "Remember to **rest** on the sabbath." Jesus tells us to come to Him all who are weary and carry heavy burdens and He will give us **rest**! Christ had a ministry that saved the world in three short years. Yet He routinely took time to **re**lax, **re**fuel, **re**flect and **re**group with His Father before He **re**turned to **re**spond to other's needs. So let the white lines on the road **re**mind you to **re**create white space in your life and **re**center your thoughts on Jesus!

# NOT GOOD TO BRING GOOD

## ROMANS 8:28-30

My father has Parkinson's Disease. He also has a sense of humor. He makes us laugh doing a jig he calls the Parkinson's shuffle. Dad says he's a "mover and a shaker."

Our heavenly father promises that: "All things will work together for good to those who love God." While God reassures us that every detail can be worked into something good, He did not say that every detail is good. Parkinson's disease is not good. Brokenness due to abuse is not good. Cancer is not good. Violence is not good. But God promises that He can and will use even those things that are not good to bring good.

If God has ever brought something good out of a circumstance that was not good, this is your testimony. Like my dad, you can be a "mover and shaker" sharing God's goodness with others.

# PERFUME AND PRAYERS

## MATTHEW 6:6

*C*ertain scents make us smile. When I smell Estee Lauder's "Beautiful," I think of my beautiful mom. When my husband smells "Sweet Honesty," he thinks of our wedding day. Perfumes evoke memories and feelings. In the Bible we're told that God remembers our prayer conversations as though they were a sweet-smelling perfume.

God cherishes our conversations because He cherishes us. No need for formalities or long, fancy prayers. In fact, one of the shortest verses in the Bible is three words: "Don't stop praying."

We're told when we pray: "The focus will shift from us to God, and we will begin to sense his **grace**." Maybe that's why prayers before meals are called grace. Meals are a way to fill our tummies with food and our spirits with gratitude. So while I may forget to wear perfume, I never forget to eat. From this day forward, may we never forget to pray.

# BEN, THE BIBLE AND F.R.O.G.S

## PROVERBS 3:5-12

*B*enjamin Franklin once said, "God helps those who help themselves."[1] Though this sounds like Ben was quoting the Bible, he was not. In fact, the Bible teaches that God helps those who trust in Him.

We're told to "Trust God from the bottom of your heart; don't try to figure out everything on your own. Listen for God's voice in everything you do, everywhere you go; He's the one who will keep you on track." When I hear this verse, I am reminded to **Fully Rely On God** or **F.R.O.G.**.

God wants us to rely on Him for help before we step out of His Will in an attempt to help ourselves. And while the Bible tells us that we are all required to work, God wants us to rely on Him for guidance. Each day we do well to say, "Thy will not my will be done."

# SHUT THE FRONT DOOR ON FEAR

## 2 TIMOTHY 1:7

*W*hen fear rings your doorbell, send faith to answer the door. Practically speaking how do we "shut the front door" on fear?

God fills us with courage promising, "I have not given you a spirit of fear, but of power and of love and of a sound mind." That's a promise that you can quote, inserting your name.

> "God has not given _____ a spirit of fear,
> but of power and of love and of a sound mind."

So when fear pounds on your door so hard it shakes the walls of your world, speak this verse out loud and send fear running!

# JORDAN AND JOSHUA

## JOSHUA 1:7-9

Over a hundred times, famed NBA champion and MVP Michael Jordan missed game-winning shots. He shares, "I've failed over and over again and that is why I succeed." Michael inspires us to "Just Do It™."

If Nike were around in Biblical times, Joshua would have been an excellent spokesman. Faith in God allows him to have the right attitude. He tells us to "Be strong and very courageous. Don't be timid; don't get discouraged. God, your God, is with you every step you take."

It's not about how many times you get knocked down. It's about how many times you get up. So no matter what brand of athletic shoes you wear, know that you have the best coach cheering you on. Truly if God is for us, who can be against us!

# POTHOLES

JOHN 16:33

My daughter is the only person I know that enjoys hitting potholes. Buckled in her car seat she lifts her hands high like she's on a roller coaster, giggling, "More, Momma. Go faster!" As adults we think about the damage to our car. Yet as I ponder the topic of potholes, I'm challenged. They're like little valleys in the road.

In the Bible we hear plenty about valleys and trials. One of my favorite passages was written by David, a shepherd-turned-king. He pens, "Even though I walk through the valley of the shadow of death, I fear no evil for God is with me."

God is better at comforting us than any shock absorbers. When we hit life's rough patches, He's with us, assuring us: "Here on earth you will have many trials and sorrows. But take heart, because I have overcome the world." With Him we can proclaim, "I can do everything through Christ, who gives me strength."

# SHOW AND TELL

## JOHN 3:16-21

*D*o you remember the wonders of Show and Tell? The exhilaration of having a special item to share with your classmates and even the disappointment of having nothing to share? In kindergarten we learned the art of showing and telling. As Christians, might we also be called to Show and Tell by showing someone our love for God with a kind deed and telling them about our kind Savior? When I look at the consistent example of Jesus throughout His ministry, He not only met people's physical needs, He met their deeper spiritual needs.

One of the most basic Bible verses is a bit like show and tell. John 3:16 shows us God's love by telling us: "For this is how God loved the world: He gave his one and only Son, so that everyone who believes in him will not perish but have eternal life." Today might you **show** someone your love for God with a kind deed and **tell** them about your Savior?

# GIRL SCOUT CAMP & GLITTER NAIL POLISH

## PROVERBS 18:4

For a homesick Girl Scout stuck at summer camp, glitter nail polish was the best gift ever. This little surprise from my big sister brought big comfort. I knew I wasn't alone in a place with mosquitos that bit and latrines that stunk. Having my sister at Camp Na-Wa-Kwa helped even if she wasn't in my same tent.

Even as adults, we face foes that bite and trials that stink. Whether we are a Girl Scout or a grown woman, we each need love and encouragement. There are so many people that are hurting and need a hug.

We are the arms of Christ's army. A little gesture can make a BIG difference. Here's the good news. You don't need glitter nail polish or glittery polished words to let others know you care. If you have arms, you are qualified to offer a hug!

# EARS DON'T HAVE LIDS

## PROVERBS 8:34-36

*E*yes have lids so that you can close them. Ears don't. Even though ears don't have lids, our kids can sure close them. Truth be known, I'm God's child and I can close my ears to Him. But this morning I heard Him loud and clear. I listen to the Daily Audio Bible app when I exercise. Today's Proverb hit home because I needed a pick-me-up.

"Joyful are those who listen to me."

That's seven words that put bounce back in my step. "Joyful are those who listen to me." If you need more joy, find more ways to listen to God. My Christian radio station helps me hear God! Spending time in creation does too. No matter where we are, we can listen to God. After all, our ears don't have lids!

# KILEY'S COURAGE

## JOHN 3:1-18

My new friend, Kiley Daniels, is eighteen years old. She looked stunning in her homecoming dress with the cute heels she found on sale. Kiley has a sweet smile and a sweet boyfriend named Cole.

What you also need to know is that Kiley has brain cancer. But cancer doesn't define Kiley. She loves life and Jesus and is wise beyond her years. Like the pair of pumps Kiley bought for prom, she understands firsthand that joy is often paired with sorrow, success with setbacks and life with loss.

In the midst of her battle with brain cancer, Kiley radiates hope and beauty as she shares her faith. She inspires me to be bold and brave as I share that, "God so loved the world that He gave his only Son, that whoever believes in Him will not die but have eternal life." Now that's a promise of a lifetime!

# MY MARRIAGE IS LIKE A HYBRID CAR

## EPHESIANS 5:21-33

*M*y marriage has a lot in common with my hubby's hybrid. Like his car that is fueled by electricity and gas, I am fueled by love while my husband is fueled by respect. We each have different strengths and weaknesses, yet together we complement each other. Cooperatively we can solve problems, just like a hybrid solves both energy and emission problems.

When my husband and I communicate with love and respect, our words can sound and feel so different. Likewise, hybrid cars compared to traditional cars can sound and feel so different.

We have found love and respect allows our communication to be more efficient with less harmful emissions, like hybrid cars. So here's to love and respect fueling our communication and our marriages!

# COKE® AND CHRIST

JOHN 4:7-26

"I'd like to teach the world to sing in perfect harmony.
I'd like to buy the world a Coke® and keep it company."

*B*ack in 1971 this ad for Coke struck a chord. Even today we want a world at peace in perfect harmony. This tune brings to mind a story about two African men who carried a case of Coke® on foot between them ten miles just to sit with a missionary. She was mourning the loss of her grandfather. Coke® was her favorite drink and it cost them two days wages. As they sat with her, she told them about Christ, so that they, like her granddad, could live in heaven. Though Coke® can never satiate our thirst, Christ can. What the world wants is *The Real Thing.*

Christ is *The Real Thing.*

130

# WORK AND WORSHIP

## COLOSSIANS 3:23-24

*W*ork and Worship. We work six days a week and we worship on the seventh, right? But what if your work could truly become your worship. Then every day would be holy and a bit more like a holy day or as we say holi-day.

Whether we are a bookkeeper or a street sweeper like my dad, our work might be more enjoyable. We would make more than money, we would make a difference.

The Bible tells us, "Whatever you do, work at it with all your heart as though you were working for the Lord and not for people." That's my prayer…that every work day becomes worship.

# BIBBIDI-BOBBIDI-BOO

## JOHN 14:12-14

*M*y daughter's favorite line from Cinderella is spoken by the fairy Godmother who says the magic words:

"Salaga doola, Menchicka boola, Bibbidi-bobbidi-boo!"

Lately when I ask Alyssa to say the "magic word," instead of thank you, she coyly offers, "Bibbidi-bobbidi-boo!" This makes me think, sometimes we try to use "magic words" when we pray. The Bible teaches us to pray "in Jesus's name." But that's more than a **tagline**. Our prayers need to be **in line** with God's Word and His Will. When Jesus says we can ask for anything, our asking must be in His name–that is according to God's character and will. For me, a better prayer is for His perfect will in my imperfect life saying, "Thy will not my will be done."

# A DIM LIGHT BULB

## LAMENTATIONS 3:22-26

Ten watts is all that's needed to power a dim lightbulb. Our brain uses the same amount of power as a ten-watt bulb. That's efficient. And what's more amazing is that our brain has the potential to store 2.5 million Gigabytes or 300 years worth of TV. That's all the information that's on the internet. Talk about mind-blowing. And yet I struggle to memorize the Bible. Over the years, I found that repetition helps me remember. So when I'm doing something repetitive, like walking, it helps me wear memory paths in my brain.

Yesterday while walking I memorized, "We walk by faith, not by sight." This morning I memorized, "Great is His faithfulness. His mercies are new every morning." I don't always remember where to find them in the Bible, but then again I don't always remember where to find my cell phone. God understands that we are works in progress and He is patient with us.

# LAUNDRY AND LOVE

## 1 CORINTHIANS 13:4-13

*I*t's easy to feel lost between loads of dirty dishes and dirty socks. Our families repeatedly grow hungry and need to be fed. And dirty clothes fill our hampers, but our hearts don't need to be hampered and heavy because what we do in love has lasting effects.

Service done in love in God's name to care for others doesn't disappear like food in the fridge or socks in the dryer. No. God credits love to our eternal account.

How do I know? It's a truth I cherish from 1 Corinthians 13:13. "Three things will last forever-faith, hope and love- and the greatest of these is love." When we love God and love others, we've done well! Love is eternal. Laundry only seems to last forever.

# DRY CISTERNS

## JEREMIAH 2:13

My family gets our water from a cistern that is filled monthly. Once I left the hose running watering new shrubs and ran the cistern dry. The timing was horrible as we had out-of-town family arriving and not a drop of water. That day I felt firsthand what I've often felt spiritually. Feeling empty and dry happens to us all. When I don't make time for Jesus, my soul feels sun-baked. I'm short-tempered and shortsighted. I feel less joy and more frustration.

Sometimes I turn to spiritually "dry cisterns." Food doesn't satiate my starved soul. Shopping doesn't satisfy my spirit. Facebook leaves me facedown. Television fills my time, but it doesn't fill my mind with things that are true and honorable. Instead of being a warrior fighting for good, I become a worrier thinking the worst. But the Good News is, we can cry out to Jesus and run to Him for Living Water. His cistern never runs dry.

# CAP'N CRUNCH

## 2 CORINTHIANS 4:8-18

*O*ne minute my daughter was staring up at the box of Cap'n Crunch and the next her little brother came barreling down the aisle full speed. BANG. Then Alyssa was being dragged like a Swifter® mop pinned under the cart. Her sweet hands gripped the bar that forced her chin backward collapsing her windpipe. My little girl looked up at me in shock.

Are there times in life when one moment you're standing upright and the next you feel like you're run over by life? While I don't have all the answers, like my daughter clung to the bottom bar of the cart, during trials I cling to promises like: "We are pressed on every side by troubles, but we are not crushed...We get knocked down, but we are not destroyed." These truths encourage me to hang. I'm grateful they're from the King of all Kings, not sugarcoated promises made by a fictitious guy named Cap'n Crunch.

# MOUNTAIN DEW® & HOT MESSY LIVES

## 1 PETER 4:12-19

My guilty pleasure is Mountain Dew and I just learned that it contains BMO or Brominated Vegetable Oil which is also a flame retardant. This makes me rethink my choice of caffeine. I have to admit that drinking a flame retardant isn't nearly as appealing as being flame retardant.

The Bible tells me when hot trials hit "don't jump to the conclusion that God isn't on the job. Instead, be glad that you're in the very thick of what Christ experienced. This is a spiritual refining process, with glory just around the corner."

Like Daniel's friends–Shadrach, Meshach, and Abednego–who were thrown in the fiery furnace, we too can survive and thrive. We don't need to drink Mountain Dew to be flame retardant, but we do need Christ. Let's invite Him into our hot messy lives today.

# BROKEN BABY JESUS & MR. ELMER

## COLOSSIANS 3:2

*W*hen my daughter was almost two, she kidnapped baby Jesus from the nativity manger. Dragging her rocking chair into the kitchen, Alyssa swaddled Jesus in a washcloth. Then the unthinkable happened. Alyssa dropped Him and His head broke off. If Jesus were in my kitchen watching my toddler, He would have been touched by her kindness. He came to Earth to be a living sacrifice broken *for* her. To have the figurine of Him quite literally broken **by** her is a reminder of the price He paid out of love.

When our days are filled with broken dreams and broken hearts, He encourages us to think about "the things of heaven, not the things of earth." On earth there will always be brokenness. In heaven all brokenness will be healed, not just glued back together with a bottle of Elmer's. What broken moments might you entrust to Him today?

# BEAUTY AND GOD'S FRIDGE

## ISAIAH 49:16

*I*n the U.S. the cosmetic industry is worth 100 billion dollars.[1] Everyone wants to be beautiful! So this caught my eye today: "Beautiful eyes look for the good in others and beautiful lips speak words of kindness." When others find the good in us and lift us up with kind compliments, our world is more beautiful.

Searching for good and granting others grace, that's what God does for us. God's crazy about us. In fact, if God had a fridge, I think our drawing would be on it. And if God had a cell phone, I believe our picture would be His screen saver. Why? God tells us "On the palms of my hands, I have written your name." So no matter how bad your day is, know that you are beautiful and you are loved.

# TRASH TO TREASURE

## PHILIPPIANS 1:3-6

As the old adage goes: "What's one gal's trash is another gal's treasure." I was raised shopping at garage sales. To this day I love to find deals that are steals then take and make second-hand finds into lovely pieces.

Some might say it's because I grew up poor, but I believe God gave me the gift to see potential in people and projects. God helps me take what is broken and make it beautiful. This is my testimony.

The Bible tells us that God doesn't make junk, assuring us that we are "fearfully and wonderfully made." And that "God who began a good work in us will bring it to completion." We aren't like a Pinterest project gone bad. (I know because I've had plenty of those.) We are "created anew every day for good works." You and I are not any man's trash. We are God's treasure.

# IMPERFECT LIFE~PERFECT GOD

## EPHESIANS 3:16-19

*L*ately our world has been far from perfect. We all want a perfect life with a perfect marriage and perfect kids. But even God doesn't have perfect children who make perfect decisions. Together we struggle with all of humanity. Don't believe for a second that those who look like they have perfect lives on Facebook aren't facing hard things.

While there is no perfect nation, no perfect family, and no perfect job, we do have a perfect heavenly Father who loves us perfectly. He knows our mistakes—our tears and our fears—and despite our imperfections, He is our biggest supporter. And He walks beside us through this imperfect life.

So while we will never have a perfect spouse or a perfect house, with Christ as our Savior, we can look forward to an eternity of perfect joy!

# LAUGHTER AND TEARS

## JOHN 10:10

*L*aughter and tears. Joy and sorrow. Mountain tops and valleys. They are like peanut butter and jelly. They go together in this sandwich called life.

Experiencing one gives height and depth to the other. Joy is not the absence of sorrow. And sorrow is not the absence of joy. (That's worth re-reading.) In this life we are told we will have many sorrows but we also will have abundant joy.

I think Jesus was the type of guy that knew both. He wept but He also feasted. In fact, He was called a glutton, a drunkard and a friend to tax collectors and other sinners. Jesus makes no apology for resting and rejoicing. In fact, He tells us that He came that we might have abundant life and life to the fullest. So even in sorrows we can find simple joys. A simple joy for me is a simple peanut butter and jelly sandwich.

# ROUTINES THAT ROOT

## 1 THESSALONIANS 3:11-13

*a*tree's roots should mirror its branches. In order to be well-girded for life's storms, we too need welldeveloped roots. Our faith, family and friends serve as our roots.

It's hard to make time for routines that root us and to make time for quiet time…to press pause and pray rather than press on and fray. Sometimes it's the small things that can make a BIG difference.

Growing up we would kneel down beside our bed each night as a family. Lately I revived this small tradition, but with a morning twist. I slip out of bed and slip to my knees, thanking God for the day and committing my walk to Him. Then I head to the kitchen to slip a tea bag in hot water to infuse it with flavor while I infuse my mind reading my Bible. What routines root your life?

# CALMING STORMS

MARK 4:35-41

Sometimes Jesus calms the storm around us. Sometimes he lets the storms rage on and he calms the storm inside us. It's tornado season in Kansas City. We know about storms and we remember the story of the twelve disciples who got caught in a fierce storm on the Sea of Galilee while Jesus slept.

What I didn't remember is that the boat was actually filling with water. Sometimes we too are in grave danger of drowning. During those times it's comforting to know that Jesus isn't just in our boat, His Holy Spirit is living within us. This allows us to experience a peace that surpasses human understanding.

More often than miraculously calming the storms of life *around* me, the Holy Spirit calms the storm *inside* me so I can experience Christ in the chaos rather than the Devil in the details.

# THE MIDDLE CHILD

## HEBREWS 6:13-20

*E*ven in today's throw away economy, "Three things will last forever: **faith, hope** and **love** and the greatest of these is love." If hope were personified, she would be the middle child sandwiched between faith and love. Faith would be the big sister, who leads the way. And love would be the little sister, who steals our hearts. Like a middle child, hope can be overshadowed and taken for granted until we have none.

Hope stabilizes us. The Bible tells us, "This hope is a strong and trustworthy anchor for our souls. It leads us through the curtain into God's inner sanctuary." Hope isn't meant just for heaven. Hope leads us into God's presence and helps us run the race in the here and now. Let's place our hope in Christ today. Hope is always uplifting!

# GOOD LUCK

## DEUTERONOMY 30:2-10

*W*hen wishing someone well, we commonly say, "Good luck." Today I learned the meaning behind the phrase. It began in ancient Greece. Luck is the English name for the Greek goddess named Tyche. She was worshipped in hopes of gaining good fortune.[1] This gives me cause to pause and ask if my words imply that I have faith in a false Greek god.

Matthew tells us that what we say with our mouths is a reflection of what we believe in our hearts. Since I put my faith in God alone, I would rather say "God bless you" than "good luck."

God wants to bless people and has given us the ability to speak, knowing that our words can tear down or build up. Our words are tools in a sculptor's hand. Who might you build up today with a kind word or heartfelt compliment?

# FLAT TIRES AND GOD

## ROMANS 8:35-39

*H*aving a flat tire just lets the air out of my day. Recently my pastor shared that the unexpectedness of a flat tire reminded him of how suddenly things can change. Covid 19 flattened the world's tires. We saw signs in peoples' yards that said, "God's Got This." But Pastor Mike reminded us that compared to the power of God, coronavirus is no more challenging than a flat tire. No worries, "God's Got This."

This got Mike thinking perhaps a better sign would say, "God's Got **Us**." Nothing can separate **us** from the love of God. It is Christ Jesus who intercedes for us at the right hand of God so that no hardship, distress, persecution, famine, nakedness, peril, sword or worldwide pandemic will separate us from the love of God in Jesus Christ. We will all have disappointments, but we will never be without God. "God's Got Us."

# MEPHIBO...WHAT?

## 2 SAMUEL 9

ephibosheth. It's a hard name to pronounce and he had a hard life. It started well as he was born into royalty but went downhill quick when he was crippled by a fall. Mephibosheth was King Saul's grandson who was granted grace by King David. Typically the family of an overthrown king would be put to death, but David treated Mephibosheth as a beloved son. He became part of David's family and was invited to eat at the king's table for the rest of his life.

Why is Mephibosheth's story told in the Bible? Because he represents us. Like Mephibosheth, we too were born into royalty as a child of the King. Like Mephibosheth, we too have survived a fall that has left us crippled. Like Mephibosheth, we too are invited to our King's banqueting table for all eternity. And like Mephibosheth, we too are imperfect, but we are perfectly loved.

# YOU'RE EXTRAORDINARY

## GENESIS 1:27-31

*Y*ou may feel ordinary, no more special than a droplet of rain in a storm. But I'm here to tell you that you're extraordinary in God's eyes. How do I know? God tells me in the first chapter of the Bible. After creating you and me, He says that we are "good, very good."

But we look in the mirror and see our blemishes. We look at our lives and see our bent and broken moments. Yet through Christ, God looks at us and sees His unblemished children.

He looks at our bent and broken moments like raindrops that form perfect prisms, allowing us—like colorless light—to be bent and broken, blooming in arcs of color to form a rainbow. Trust Him to bring beauty from your bent and broken moments today!

# AFFLUENZA

## MATTHEW 6:19-21

*I*nfluenza is a health problem. "Affluenza" is a spiritual problem and it's highly contagious. We've lived thru a worldwide pandemic and understand firsthand how important vaccines can be. The good news is that we have a vaccine for "Affluenza." The Bible calls it generosity. We don't need bigger houses with bigger closets and bigger garages, we need bigger hearts with bigger visions. 2 Corinthians 9:6-8 reminds us that: "Whoever sows sparingly will also reap sparingly, and whoever sows **generously** will also reap **generously**...for God loves a cheerful giver." Jesus Himself tells us not to store up treasures here on earth but rather store treasures up in heaven where moths and rust cannot destroy. Wherever your treasure is your heart will also be. I want my heart to be focused on heaven and Jesus. Wealth and health are fleeting but being with Jesus in heaven is forever.

# FRIENDS

## JOHN 15:12-16

*I*n the Old Testament Moses is the only person who is called a friend of God. While I often think of myself and others as God's children, I don't think of being God's friend. But today I was reading the book of John where Jesus says, "This is my command: Love one another the way I loved you. This is the very best way to love. Put your life on the line for your friends. You are my friends when you do the things I command you."

Jesus commands us to love God and love others. When we do this, we are His friends. We also find ourselves with more friends because we treat others as we would like to be treated. So if you're having a down day, perhaps knowing that Jesus counts you as His friend will bring bounce back to your step. Everyone needs authentic friends who love like Jesus.

# THE TIGER AND THE TONGUE

JAMES 3:9-12

Words are powerful. The more years I spend walking with God, the more I'm convinced that choosing Godly words is one of the most difficult spiritual disciplines. Apparently James did too. He explains, "You can tame a tiger, but you can't tame a tongue—it's never been done. With our tongues we bless God then with the same tongues we curse the very men and women he made in his image."

As a mom, I want my words to reinforce positive characteristics that I see in my kids. When they pick up their toys, I tell them what diligent workers they are becoming. When they ask questions, I tell them how smart they are to look for answers. When they speak with kindness, I tell them how loving others brings God glory. When they listen and then obey, I tell them how proud I am they act without murmuring or complaining. How might you shape the world today with your words?

# FAITH AND "THE SHOW ME STATE"

## HEBREWS 11:1-6

*B*elieve it or not, you are singled out and given a verbal pat on the back in the Bible by Jesus Himself! He references you and me when appearing to Thomas after His resurrection saying, "blessed are they that have not seen, and yet have believed." Living in "The **Show** Me State" of Missouri, we say "seeing is believing." But Hebrews 11 tells us that, "Faith **shows** the reality of what we hope for; it is the evidence of **things we cannot see.** Through their faith, the people in days of old earned a good reputation. By faith we understand that the entire universe was formed at God's command, that what we now see did not come from anything that can be seen." We are told, "Without faith it is impossible to please God." So how do we build our faith? Romans 10:17 tells us, "Faith comes from hearing, that is, hearing the Good News about Christ." You're building your faith right now!

# YABBA DABBA DOO

## JOHN 10:25-30

Fred Flintstone says, "Yaba-daba-do!" We recognize Fred by his voice, but do we always recognize our Good Shepherd by His voice? The cool thing about sheep is that they know their shepherd's voice and only follow him. Sheep from many shepherds may sleep mixed together in the same enclosure, but when the gate is opened in the morning, they're easily separated. All a shepherd has to do is call his flock out of the pen by calling them to follow him into the pasture.

Jesus is our Good Shepherd and He wants us to follow Him. Sometimes we hear competing voices that are loud like T.V. commercials. Those voices that tell us to keep up with the Jones's. They tell us we only have worth if we are beautiful. But that's not what our Good Shepherd tells us. Let's spend time with Jesus so we know His voice and can follow Him, experiencing life to the fullest!

# CHOCOLATE CHIP COOKIES AND LIFE

JOHN 16:33

*W*hen you divide a warm chocolate chip cookie, no one complains when their half has more chips. Just as no one complains when they get a good break of the cookie, no one complains when they get a good break in life. But when we get the bad break and are told, "That's just how the cookie crumbles," it's a different story. We grumble, "Life's not fair."

Yet Jesus reassures us, saying, "I have told you all this so that you may have peace in me. Here on earth you will have many trials and sorrows. But take heart, because I have overcome the world."

Assuredly we will have bad breaks in life. And life won't always be fair. But even when bad breaks happen, God will work all things together for our good. That's a promise better than any cookie.

# ESCALATORS

GALATIANS 5:22-26

*P*icture this. You're climbing up an escalator that's going down and, hard as you try, you can't reach the top. Some days life feels exhausting like climbing up an escalator the wrong way.

An escalator is to help us climb easier. Likewise, the Holy Spirit is to help us press onward and upward. The Bible tells us that the Spirit moves us to be more loving, more joyful, more peaceful and more patient. With the Holy Spirit living in us we can be kinder, more faithful, gentler and more spirit-controlled.

So on days you feel like you're going the wrong way on an escalator, press pause rather than press on and ask for the Holy Spirit's help. With the Spirit empowering us, we can reach new heights.

# THE HAPPIEST VS. THE BEST

GENESIS 50:19-21

*I* recently read that the happiest people in the world don't necessarily **have** the best of everything, they just **make** the best of everything. This reminds me of Joseph. He was sold by his brothers into slavery and dragged to Egypt. There he was wrongly accused, imprisoned and seemingly forgotten for years.

But God didn't forget Joseph. He was released from prison and rose to power to keep nations from dying of starvation. And Joseph forgave his brothers, exclaiming, "What you intended for evil, God intended for good."

As Christians, we can be the the most joyful people in the world not be cause we **have** the best of everything but because we know that God can **make** the best of everything working all things together for our good.

# PARESTHESIA

## ROMANS 7:15-20

oday I sat at my desk so long my leg went numb. It's a strange feeling when your foot falls asleep. When you cut off the leg's blood supply you cause what doctors call "paresthesia." There is a spiritual lesson to be learned from this. Just as our extremities may feel numb from lack of blood flow, we may feel numb from lack of connection to God.

Emotional numbness temporarily immobilizes us just as physical numbness does. Though we may look the same outwardly, we can be numb to our blessings, our family and friends. Just as we can stomp our foot when it's asleep, we can stomp through our day devoid of delight. While numbness lasts only minutes, God's love is eternal. So the next time your foot falls asleep might you be reminded to walk in love?

# BIGGER AND BETTER

## JEREMIAH 31:13

*R*emember the scavenger hunt game of Bigger and Better? You start off with something small and trade it for something Bigger and Better. I remember winning when my team started with a safety pin and won with a king-size mattress. We're never too old for the game of Bigger and Better. When we knock on God's door in prayer, He's like a good neighbor who is all in and wants us to win. He offers to trade our safety-pin-sorrows for king-size joys. He'll gladly trade our worries for His peace that passes understanding. He'll exchange our bitterness for bigger and better Love. And the best part is that He invites us to be a Bigger and Better part of the game by blessing others. We can be that fun neighbor who gives Bigger and Better smiles in exchange for scowls…or compliments instead of complaints. I'm all in…are you?

# CINNAMON ROLLS AND ANGELS

## HEBREWS 13:1-6

*W*arm cinnamon rolls covered with gooey icing are so yummy. Cinnamon rolls remind me of my grandma who served them whenever she entertained. I still remember the story she told about my dad. As a toddler he once secretly licked the icing off the rolls in the kitchen while she greeted guests in the front room. This memory popped into my mind this morning as I popped cinnamon rolls in the oven. They were from the ordinary cardboard roll I bought in the refrigerator section of the grocery store. I wasn't entertaining guests, just my family. In the Bible where we're told to: "Keep on loving each other. Don't forget to show hospitality to strangers, for some who have done this have entertained angels without realizing it!" This reminds me that I serve both those in my home and those who don't have a home. What can you do today that's *ordinary* but may seem *extraordinary*, even angelic, to someone?

# THE PURPOSE OF LIFE

## EPHESIANS 2:10

*W*e often hear, "The purpose of life is a life of purpose." But what gives life purpose? God's Word tells us that we are created to bring Him glory. "We are his workmanship, created in Christ Jesus for good works." Doing good in Jesus's name brings God glory and that's our purpose.

Sometimes I make it way too complicated but Jesus kept it simple, saying, "Love God and love others." When we do this, we are living our purpose and have a life of purpose.

In fact, we can impact eternity when we love others sharing the Good News. How do I know? The Bible tells us faith, hope and love last forever and the greatest of these are love. So live a life of great purpose and love someone well today.

# TEARS AND FEARS

## PSALM 56:8

The older I get the more I forget! During the COVID quarantine of 2020 everything was a blur. I forgot what day of the week it was constantly. Though we may forget, I'm so grateful that God remembers those things that are important to us.

Today I was reading Psalms and was reminded that God remembers all my sorrows and even collects my tears. Even if others don't see our tears and our fears, God does.

God knows what hurts our hearts. Our tears are precious to Him. Even better, He tells us that a day is coming when He will wipe every tear from our eyes and there will be no more death or sorrow or crying or pain. Having just lived through this pandemic, it's encouraging to know that the best is yet to come in heaven! As Billy Graham reminds us, "The moment we take our last breath on earth, we take our first in heaven."[1]

# HOPE AND OXYGEN

## MICAH 7:7

$S$ome say that hope is a *wish*. But with Christ we can do so much more than just *wish*. The Bible teaches that faith is built on past experiences, while hope is focused on future experiences. It seems to me that when faith steps into the future, she becomes hope, being both mature and certain.

Without hope, we're left with a flimsy, whimsy wish that leaves us breathless, longing for more. But when we connect to Christ in faith, He infuses us with hope. We can breathe in hope then exhale fear.

Hope in Christ oxygenates our souls so we can say, like Micah, "As for me, I look to the Lord for help. I wait confidently for God to save me, and my God will certainly hear me." The world needs to hear this message of hope: God hears us and He saves us.

# SUNSHINE

## MATTHEW 5:14-16

Strange as it sounds, not all light in the electromagnetic spectrum is visible. Infrared and ultraviolet light can't be seen by the naked eye. Yet even in the darkest conditions, there are tiny bits of light present. Likewise, even in our darkest days, God provides light.

Sometimes when I wake up weighed down, in addition to my Bible and prayer, I need a visible friend to help me see the blessings in my life. Some friends have that ability to make you feel like sunshine.

We're told to be light to the world, "like a city on a hilltop that cannot be hidden...to let our good deeds shine out for all to see, so that everyone will praise our heavenly Father." Our good deeds bring visible light to others. Who might you shine on today?

# HIDE AND SEEK

## LUKE 15:8-10

When playing Hide and Seek outside Jerusalem, a young girl hid in the old trunk of a hollowed-out olive tree. There she found a gold coin! It predated Christ and was worth so much, she built her family a home with it.

Recently I lost the most expensive gift I had ever been given, my gold tennis bracelet. While it wasn't worth as much as the coin, it was priceless to me. So I asked God what He'd have me find through this loss. What He taught me was to find and enjoy priceless moments with Him, family and friends.

Imagine how many hidden moments of gratitude we could find if we were seeking them. Let's greet each day with child-like excitement, proclaiming, "Ready or not here I come!"

# POISON IVY

## PHILIPPIANS 4:6-7

*P*oison ivy is the worst. I've learned, "Leaves of three, let them be." And, "Red leaflets in spring are a dangerous thing." Or, "A hairy vine is no friend of mine." Even, "Side leaflets like mittens will itch like the dickens." While I can now identify poisonous plants, I'm still no expert at identifying weeds.

In the parable of the sower Jesus talks about weedy worries that choke us. He tells us that when we're worried, the result will be no fruit. Not the kind we eat, like kiwi and kumquats, but the kind we possess, like peace and patience. So if you need a spiritual Weed Be Gone® for worry try this promise: "Don't worry about anything; instead, pray about everything. Tell God what you need and thank him for all he has done!" God doesn't want us to get stuck in the weeds!

# GET UP DON'T GIVE UP

## I CORINTHIANS 9:24-26

et up don't give up. That's easier said than done. Some days we feel empowered. Other days we feel exhausted. On those days I am drained, I need more than a shot of espresso. I need a shot of spiritual enkephalins and endorphins.

Like a champion coach Paul cheers us on, saying, "Don't you realize that in a race everyone runs, but only one person gets the prize? So run to win! All athletes are disciplined in their training. They do it to win a prize that will fade away, but we do it for an eternal prize. So run with purpose in every step." With verses like these I'm inspired to GET UP don't GIVE UP.

# MAC & CHEESE OR STRAINED PEAS

## REVELATION 22:1-5

*W*hat was your favorite food as a kid? Mine was orange macaroni and cheese in the blue box. My son's favorite food is Gerber's® strained peas. No salt. No butter. Just room temperature smashed peas. In fact, when he sees the the jar he starts clapping his hands and kicking his feet so hard his high chair rocks. From Garrett's perspective, smashed peas are scrumptious.

We gag at the thought.

My tastes are different as a grown-up. This provides me with perspective on how my "tastes" will change when I experience the wonders of heaven. Whatever your favorite food, I suspect that none will taste as perfect as what we experience in heaven. Today as you journey forward, enjoy a food you love and let it remind you that the most scrumptious stuff is yet to come.

# BRACH'S® CHOCOLATE STARS

## PSALM 116:15-19

*O*ne of the sweetest childhood memories of my uncle was the sweet secret we shared. In the bottom drawer of his clothes chest, he had a bag of Brach's Milk Chocolate Stars®.

Uncle Don would wink and motion for me to scamper past Aunt Martha in the kitchen. When he would ask how many stars I wanted, I could hardly swallow my giggles. By golly I wanted as many as my little hands could hold.

Though I don't see bags of Brach's Stars® often, I do see stars in the night sky and think of him often. He always called me "Precious" so today I'm comforted by the Biblical promise, "Precious in the sight of the Lord is the death of his saints." What sweet memories can help you through the loss of someone precious?

# SHORT & SWEET

## 1 THESSALONIANS 5:16-18

*I*n the Bible we're told to: "Never stop praying." That's three words and it's nearly the shortest verse in the Bible. We're told that when we pray: "The focus will shift from us to God, and we will begin to sense his grace." Prayer helps us walk focused on Him in His Will.

Each time we pray "The Lord's Prayer," we're praying God's Will for our lives be done on earth as His will is done in heaven. We're asking for our daily bread, for the grace, strength and direction to walk in His Will. And we appeal to God asking that He leads us away from temptation. When we align our will with His, God can keeps us from evil.

God remembers our prayer conversations as though they were a sweet-smelling perfume. So today when you smell something good, be reminded that your prayers are wonderfully pleasant to God, who loves you dearly!

# WINES AND VINES

## JOHN 15:1-4

*L*iving in Kansas City, we're known for our steaks more than our grapes so I'm less familiar with wines and vines. In the parable of the vineyard Jesus says that He is the grapevine and His Father is our Gardener. We're told to stay connected to Christ, the vine, so that we can produce fruit. Knowing exactly what we need, God will prune us so that we produce even more fruit.

There were times in my life when I was pruned. While it didn't feel good at the time, looking back I can see that God knew exactly what He was doing. Might there be things in your life that need pruned so that you will produce more fruit, bringing God more glory?

# PETER, PAUL AND US

ROMANS 12:6-8

*a*n old hymn reminds us: "If you can't preach like Peter or pray like Paul, just tell the love of Jesus who died to save us all."[1] Though only a deaf skunk would appreciate my singing, this old hymn inspires me to share the Good News. In this world there's plenty of bad news for sure.

People are starved for Good News. We can share our own good news about how has Jesus has touched our life. That's "our story" and we can reach people that others simply can't. So let's share our story and share God's love. I'll never be able to preach like Peter, but I can cook a mean meatball. Add spaghetti and a salad and I can feed a family who needs to know they are loved. What are you good at and enjoy doing? And most importantly, how can you use those blessings to be a blessing to those around you? We each can make a difference leaving a lasting legacy of love!

# TEMPORARY TRIALS AND ETERNAL TIARAS

JAMES 1:12-18

*I*'ve heard many people say that a setback sets you up for a comeback. We grow through what we go through. While setbacks are hard, the Bible encourages us, saying, "Blessed is the one who perseveres under trial because having stood the test that person will receive the crown of life."

This is so like God. He rewards our **temporary trials** with **eternal tiaras**. I'll leave the debate about heavenly crowns to earthly scholars with degrees that are higher and holier than mine. I think we all agree that crowns, whether literal or figurative, are a blessing.

So rather than talkback, cutback, pullback, or fallback, this encourages me to back up and see setbacks from God's perspective. Setbacks are an opportunity to come back stronger in my faith. After all, we **grow** through what we **go** through.

# GREENER GRASS

## 1 CORINTHIANS 13

We've all done it. We look at other people and think the grass is greener on their side of the fence. But the grass is not greener just on their side. The grass is greener wherever it has been watered.

Envy is easy. Watering our own relationships is hard. Envy is like crabgrass. It can take over and ruin both our lawns and our lives. So how do we get rid of envy? We sow seeds of gratefulness. Then we water it with love.

The Bible tells us: "Love is patient and kind. Love is not jealous or boastful or proud or rude. It does not demand its own way. It is not irritable, and it keeps no record of being wronged. Love never gives up, never loses faith, is always hopeful, and endures through every circumstance." Loving others well results in lives that are greener no matter what side of the fence we live on!

# SPEED BUMPS IN THE ROAD OF LIFE

## MATTHEW 25:31-46

*U*psets. Setbacks. Setups. And strikeouts. We all have things that drive us bonkers and people that make us crazy. When frustration strikes, do we strike out or do we come out swinging?

Over the years I've found it helpful to frame frustrations with this question: "When I stand before God's throne, will this be a topic of conversation?" If the answer is no, then I tell myself, "This is just a speed bump in the road of life. It may slow me down, but it won't knock me down."

Speed bumps serve a purpose. And frustrations can serve a purpose. They can slow us down and help us to remember what will be important when we stand before God's throne. Eternal perspective helps us keep our head in the game when frustrations come out of left field.

# GOD'S FAMILY TREE AND EMBARRASSING BRANCHES

## ROMANS 5:1-6

*E*very family tree has embarrassing branches. While we might all wish for a family tree adorned with halos and harps, Jesus embraces imperfect people. How do I know? Just look at His family tree.

Abraham lied to save his hide. Jacob was so crooked he swindled his brother with beans in a bowl then hoodwinked his dad with hair from a goat. King David couldn't be trusted with wandering eyes and multiple wives. While David was a great king, he was a bad dad. And Rahab went thru rehab, trading prostitution for restitution.

Romans 5:6 tells us that, "When we were utterly helpless, Christ came at just the right time and died for us sinners." He doesn't expect us to be perfect, He just wants us to have faith in His perfect Son so that we can be grafted into His imperfect family tree.

# IRON+COPPER=BRONZE

## ECCLESIASTES 4:12

Fiftieth wedding anniversaries are celebrated by giving gold. My hubby and I have a long way to go for the gold. Interestingly, six-year anniversaries are celebrated by giving **iron**. Seven-year anniversaries by giving **copper** and eight-year anniversaries by giving **bronze**. I love this because bronze is a combination of iron and copper.

Bronze is strong like iron, but it is enduring like copper that doesn't rust. While iron and copper are both good, together they are stronger and can endure more. Like bronze, the Bible tells us that, "A person standing alone can be attacked and defeated, but two can stand back-to-back and conquer. Three are even better, for a triple-braided cord is not easily broken." When we include God in our marriage and our friendships, those relationships are more enduring. Standing alone is hard. Who can you befriend today?

# DISEASE, DEMENTIA & THE DIPPER

## JOHN 11:1-4

The Big Dipper points us toward the North Star and to God's glory. So do raindrops and rainbows. But what about diseases and dementia?

For a dozen years my dad has suffered from Parkinson's Disease and dementia. Through it all my mom has cared for him. They've been married over 60 years, and even though he doesn't always remember who she is, she tucks him in bed every night and together they pray, "Our Father who art in heaven, hallowed be thy name..."

God is "hallowed" or honored when we serve others. The Big Dipper ladles out God's glory as does my mom in every unseen act of love. So yes, even disease and dementia like the Big Dipper, can point us toward God.

# BLESSED ARE THE BUSY

## MATTHEW 5:3-10

The most quoted sermon in the history of mankind is Jesus's Sermon on the Mount. In it He gave us eight beatitudes but we often add a ninth:

Blessed are the busy.

We equate busyness with blessedness. It's so easy to get caught up in the hustle and bustle. Heaven forbid we rest or our homes may become a hot mess. But God tells us to come to Him all who are weary and carry heavy burdens and He will give us rest.

Rest is a gift from God. Being busy isn't a badge of holy honor. So stop running and start resting in His love. After all, "Blessed are the poor in Spirit." Those who depend on the Holy Spirit and His strength to meet their needs will be blessed.

# CHEERLEADERS AND CHILDREN

## EPHESIANS 2:7-10

*E*very kid dreams of what they want to be when they grow up. Underneath my 1st grade school picture sporting crooked bangs and my new too-big-for-my-face front teeth Mrs. Beasley wrote my dream on blue construction paper: "Lisa wants to be a cheerleader."

Even then God knew that I would be a cheerleader–not for a sports team–but for my family. As parents and teachers we cheer for children every day. Ephesians 2 tells us that God has us where He wants us at this very moment in our lives. He showers us with grace and kindness so that we can share it with others.

He created each of us to do kind deeds. So let's share the **kind**ness we learned in **kind**ergarten joining God in the kind work He does. No matter what your profession, we can all be cheerleaders encouraging others on today!

# KEYBOARDS AND LIVES

## ROMANS 8:28

While typing today, I realized how much the keys on our keyboards have in common with days in our lives. With old typewriters keys were once arranged in alphabetical order. The faster we typed the more metal wands became stuck together when striking the paper. So manufactures rearranged the keys to slow us down.

Sometimes God allows trials to rearrange our lives and slow us down. Although these are hard and don't initially make sense to us (like mixed up keys on a keyboard), slowing down could result in a good change. When these setbacks point us toward God, He can work them together for our good so we come back stronger. He is always uplifting, working even bad things together for our good.

# NICKNAMES

## ROMANS 8:14-17

We all have nicknames. Although my given name is Elizabeth, everyone calls me Lisa. But my most loved name is "mom." For years my daughter didn't know that my actual name was Elizabeth, because she just knew me as Mom. As we learn more about God, we learn that He has many names too. Jehovah Jireh means "the Lord my provider (Genesis 22:8)." Jehovah Rapha means "the Lord my healer (Psalm 30:2)." Jehovah Shammah means "the Lord is there (Ezekiel 48:35)." Jehovah Nissi means "the Lord is my banner or covering (Exodus 17:15)."

When Jesus taught us how to pray, He told us to call God, "our Father." The Bible tells us that God has adopted us as His children and has given us His Spirit. When we are afraid, we are told to cry out "Abba" or Daddy. I'm so grateful we have a Dad who is a pillar of strength when we are a puddle of tears.

# SPATULAS AND SPATS

## 1 CORINTHIANS 4:8

Toddlers are so funny. My nephew, Sebastian, forms attachments to random things. His all-time favorite is a spatula. While most kids have toys, Sebastian carries his spatula everywhere he goes. This makes me think. How often do we latch on to random things-like a comment from a coworker, a frown from a friend or a spat with our spouse?

The Bible provides an alternative. It tells us to, "fix our thoughts on what is true, honorable, right, pure, lovely, and admirable. Think about things that are excellent and worthy of praise." When someone compliments me or sends a positive note, I paste it into my phone notes under their name. Then when I'm having difficulty letting go of a random response, I remind myself of those compliments that are excellent and worthy of praise. Like negative thoughts, spatulas need to be left in a drawer.

# DOUBLE DECKER HORS D'OEUVRES

## JOHN 6:35-40

*A*s kids we all had our favorite snack. My mom made double-decker peanut butter and strawberry jelly sandwiches, cut into sixteenths with an extra layer of peanut butter on top. The colored tooth picks made them into fancy, fun Hors D'oeuvres. A P.B.J. sandwich may be *ordinary*, but my mom made it **extraordinary**. Do you have any foods that you make extra special with love? You probably spend a chunk of time each week buying and preparing food, then cleaning up after meals. Even driving to a restaurant and waiting to be served takes time. While good nutrition is paramount, I ask myself, "Am I more concerned with my family's physical food than their spiritual sustenance?" Do you keep a Bible in the kitchen so that you can snack on His Word? I have found a nibble here and there really adds up. So when you're waiting on your morning coffee to brew, have a bite of the Bread of Life.

# CIRCULAR RAINBOWS

## JAMES 1:2-4

God never inflicts pain or wants us to hurt, yet we do experience difficult storms. During life's storms it's hard to see how God could possibly bring good from bad. Yet ugly storms can be followed by beautiful rainbows.

We would see rainbows as complete circles if the earth didn't block the lower half of the arc.[1] In heaven we will see the complete picture. There we will better understand how trials served to complete us.

In heaven our earthly circumstances won't block our eternal vision. That's why James says, "When troubles of any kind come your way, consider it an opportunity for great joy. For you know that when your faith is tested, your endurance has a chance to grow." Rainbows are God's way of reminding us that He is completely faithful.

# RUNNING ON THE WORRY TREADMILL

## PHILIPPIANS 4:6-7

*W*orry is like running on a treadmill. It wears us out but we get nowhere fast. When I find my mind racing on the worry treadmill, I literally lace up my tennis shoes and head outside for a brisk walk and talk with my Creator.

With each step God brings to mind verses like: "Don't worry about anything; instead, pray about everything. Tell God what you need and thank him for all he has done. Then you will experience God's peace, which exceeds anything we can understand. His peace will guard your hearts and minds as you live in Christ Jesus."

Little by little God's promises nudge away worry allowing my heart to feel lighter so I have a bit more bounce in my step. Even while walking we can rest in God's promises. Physical exercise is less exhausting than running on the worry treadmill.

# A CRUDDY COLD WITH CONGESTION

## PSALM 130:5

ometimes I don't fully appreciate blessings until they're gone. For me breathing is like that. I don't realize what a gift it is to breathe freely until I can't. A cruddy cold with congestion helps me appreciate inhaling effortlessly.

I find it to be similar with hope. I can go to hopeful to hope-starved in a single breath. When I'm hungry for hope, I know where to go. I go to God.

Sometimes I find Him in a song on Christian radio. Often-times I find hope in His Word. Other times I find hope when I take a walk, inhaling fresh air with my thoughts focused on my Creator and my eyes focused on His creation. Many times I find hope in a hug from a friend who listens and cares. How can you be a friend to someone who may feel hopeless today?

# MT. RUSHMORE AND RUSHING LESS

LUKE 8:22-25

*E*ach day together through the pages of this book we have spent time with God. You have set aside time devoted to God. This is not small challenge. It's a Mt. Rushmore-sized challenge to rush less.

Rushing less...that's hard. Rushing more...as part of the human race that's what we do. The pace we face as we race from place to place is commonplace, leaving no room for rest. So here's a parting thought: Jesus became part of the human race yet He never became wrapped up in our rat race.

Not once in the Bible do we read that He hurried or rushed. In three years of ministry Jesus changed the world forever. We now keep track of time based on His birth and death. His time was short, yet he was never short on time. He could rest even in raging storms. And with Him in our boat we can too!

# CINDERELLA, ESTHER AND HAPPY ENDINGS

## ESTHER 4:13-17

*I* love books with happy endings. Perhaps that's why I love the Bible's Cinderella story about Esther. You and I have much in common with the Jewish heroine.

Esther had an imperfect life and a difficult past. She dealt with difficult people in a difficult country during difficult times. Can you relate? And Esther was adopted, just like we have been adopted into God's family. And when her adoptive father asked for her help, Esther used her position as queen to intercede to save her people.

While I am not a queen, I am a wife, a mom, a daughter, a sister and a friend. Most importantly, I am a Christian. Daily my adoptive heavenly Father asks me: "Who knows if perhaps you were made...a wife, a mom, a daughter, a sister, a friend and a Christian...for such a time as this?" Might God be calling you to intercede for someone today?

# MY SIMPLE PRAYER

## ECCLESIASTES 2:24-25

*T*oday is the oldest you've ever been...and the youngest you'll ever be again. Each day is a gift. Don't send it back unwrapped. It's easy to look forward to Friday...or payday...or holiday vacay. But how do we make every day count rather than just counting the days? Every day when I slip out of bed, I slip to my knees and simply pray:

> Lord, help me be YOUR hands and feet
> to every person that I meet
> so at the end of this day
> I have loved others YOUR way.

We can live with contagious joy so that those around us feel sunshine even when it's raining. Each day is a gift that we can share. Don't count the days. Make the days count.

# LAST WORDS

## JOHN 17:20-23

This is it. Our last devotion together. Last words are important. The last words a loved one prays are among the most cherished. Jesus's last prayer in the garden of Gethsemane was for us.

He wanted us to know, "I am praying not only for these disciples but also for all who will ever believe in me through their message. I pray that they will all be one, just as you and I are one—as you are in me, Father, and I am in you. And may they be in us so that the world will believe you sent me. I have given them the glory you gave me, so they may be one as we are one. I am in them and you are in me. May they experience such **perfect unity** that the world will know that you sent me and that you love them as much as you love me." As His church we are His stunning bride. He is standing at the end of the aisle, smiling expectantly, waiting for you!

# NOTES

## 3. MAKE A LIVING AND A LIFE

1. Quotespedia.org https://www.quotespedia.org/authors/w/winston-churchill/we-make-a-living-by-what-we-get-we-make-a-life-by-what-we-give-winston-churchill/ (accessed 2/6/2021)

## 10. A GOURMET JELLY BELLY®

1. Fabiana Buontempo and Rachel Askinasi, *How Jelly Bellys Are Made* Insider.com https://www.insider.com/behind-the-scenes-how-jelly-belly-beans-flavors-are-made-2019-10#our-company-has-been-running-continuously-since-then-8 (accessed 5/18/2020)

## 15. MOTHER-IN-LAWS AND FEAR

1. Upjourney.com https://upjourney.com/corrie-ten-boom-quotes (accessed 2/7/2021)

## 16. P.B.J.'S

1. NationalPeanutBoard.com https://www.nationalpeanutboard.org/news/who-invented-the-peanut-butter-and-jelly-sandwich.htm (accessed 2/8/2021)

## 18. CHANGING THE WORLD

1. Paulo Coelho Quotes. Goodreads.com https://www.goodreads.com/quotes/ 1003518-the-world-is-changed-by-your-example-not-by-your (accessed 2/8/2021)

## 20. BATTLES TO BLESSINGS

1. Christianity.com https://www.christianity.com/wiki/god/what-does-it-mean-that-god-is-jehovah-jireh.html (accessed 2/8/2021)

## 22. LUKEWARM LOPSIDED LOVE

1. Brynn Mannino, "9 Things You didn't Know About Starbucks," Woman's Day, online November 3, 2015. https://www.womansday.com/food-recipes/food-drinks/a1862/9-things-you-didnt-know-about-starbucks-110283/ (accessed 4/21/2020)

## 39. GUINNESS BOOK OF WORLD RECORDS AND HOPE

1. Guinness World Records Longest time breath held voluntarily (male) https://www.guinnessworldrecords.com/world-records/longest-time-breath-held-voluntarily-(male)? (accessed 2/24/2020)

## 53. SILK, STEEL & TRAILS

1. "How Strong is Silk?" Wonderopolis. Wonderopolis.org https://www.wonderopolis.org/wonder/how-strong-is-silk (accessed 4/20/2020)

## 54. GOOGLE AND GOD

1. InternetLiveStats.com     https://www.internetlivestats.com/google-search-statistics/ (accessed 2/8/2021)

## 63. WHY IS THE SKY BLUE?

1. *NASA Space Place "Why is the Sky Blue" NASA.gov* https://spaceplace.nasa.gov/blue-sky/en/ (accessed 3/3/2019)

## 99. HOW MUCH YOU CARE

1. KnowYourQuotes.com     http://www.knowyourquotes.com/People-Dont-Care-How-Much-You-Know-Until-They-Know-How-Much-You-Care-Theodore-Roosevelt.html (accessed 2/23/2021)

## 102. BRAIN FREEZE

1. MedicalNewsToday.com     https://www.medicalnewstoday.com/articles/244458 (accessed 2/9/2021)

## 115. SMALL THINGS WITH GREAT LOVE

1. MissionariesOfThePoor.org  https://missionariesofthepoor.org/doing-small-things-with-great-love2/(accessed 2/9/2021)

## 119. BEN, THE BIBLE AND F.R.O.G.S

1. CompellingTruth.org     https://www.compellingtruth.org/God-helps-those-who-help-themselves.html (accessed 2/9/2021)

## 137. BEAUTY AND GOD'S FRIDGE

1. Statista.com    https://www.statista.com/statistics/243742/revenue-of-the-cosmetic-industry-in-the-us/ (accessed 2/14/2021)

## 144. GOOD LUCK

1. Dictionary of Greek Mythology online s.v. "Aphrodite" and "Zeus," http://www.localhistories.org/greekmyths.html (accessed 3/3/2019)

## 160. TEARS AND FEARS

1. Crosswalk.com 40 Courageous Quotes from Evangelist Billy Graham https://www.crosswalk.com/faith/spiritual-life/inspiring-quotes/40-courageous-quotes-from-evangelist-billy-graham.html (accessed 3/20/21)

## 170. PETER, PAUL AND US

1. Hymnary.org                    https://hymnary.org/text/sometimes_i_feel_discouraged_spiritual (accessed 2/10/2021)

## 183. CIRCULAR RAINBOWS

1. NationalGeographic.org https://www.nationalgeographic.org/encyclopedia/rainbow/print/ (accessed 2/13/2021)

# ABOUT THE AUTHOR

Lisa Wilt is an inspirational speaker and author of multiple books. She was awarded the gold medal by Illumination Book Awards in 2019 and the silver medal in 2020. These awards honor the year's best new titles written and published with a Christian worldview. Past winners include Pope Francis, Desmond Tutu, Lysa Terkeurst and Anne Graham Lotz.

Lisa's one-minute W.O.W. Words, air daily on the radio to lighten the load for those on the go. Her blogs can be found on Life885.com. She is founder of *Rx for the Soulful Heart*, a ministry to encourage weary people and worthy ministries, with all proceeds from her speaking and books being donated to charity. You can visit her at LisaWilt.com.

For over 33 years Lisa has worked full-time as an award-winning pharmacist in community pharmacy and the pharmaceutical industry. By grace, she and her husband–a physician–have two grown children who have followed in their medical footpaths. Of all her accomplishments, the title that most defines Lisa is CHILD OF GOD. She loves making ugly duckling thrift store finds shine.

Made in the USA
Monee, IL
25 July 2021